WHEN **GOD** INTERVENES

WHEN *God* INTERVENES

An extraordinary story of faith, hope, and the power of prayer

DABNEY HEDEGARD

Tyndale House Publishers, Inc.
Carol Stream, Illinois

Visit Tyndale online at www.tyndale.com.

Visit Dabney's website at http://dabneyland.com.

When God Intervenes: An Extraordinary Story of Faith, Hope, and the Power of Prayer

Designed by Mark Anthony Lane II

Edited by Susan Taylor

Published in association with the Books & Such Literary Agency, Rachelle Gardner, 52 Mission Circle, Suite 122, PMB 170, Santa Rosa, CA 95409-5370.

Library of Congress Cataloging-in-Publication Data

Hedegard, Dabney.
  When God intervenes : an extraordinary story of faith, hope, and the power of prayer / Dabney Hedegard.
    pages cm
  ISBN 978-1-4143-7682-0 (pbk.)
1. Hedegard, Dabney—Health. 2. Lymphatics—Cancer—Complications.
3. Lymphatics—Cancer—Patients—Biography. 4. Cancer—Patients—Religious life.
5. Cancer—Religious aspects—Christianity. I. Title.
RC280.L9H43 2013
616.99'442092—dc23
[B]   2013006614

Printed in the United States of America

19 18 17 16 15 14 13
 7   6   5   4   3   2   1

To God.

Promise fulfilled. Thanks for the son.

Even at times when the Holy Ghost is moving and miracles are happening, godly men are not immune from sickness. We serve a God who heals. But we also serve a God who— as Elisha experienced, as Hezekiah experienced, as Paul makes reference to—sometimes uses sickness for his glory.

—JON COURSON

I would rather die looking for a miracle than live not believing in them.

—BILL SWEENEY

1

I scratched along my inner thigh, chasing the feather-like tickles dancing on my leg.

Then my arm.

My neck.

My stomach.

This allergic reaction—or whatever nonsense was attacking my skin—had bugged me for five months too long. Fatigued again, I slumped on my couch and mentally replayed the flurry of events from my foundation's tea earlier that afternoon: silent auction, seating arrangements, and those silly air kisses from women in spiffy hats,

1

which always made me uncomfortable. I never knew if my lips were supposed to graze their cheeks, or if my half-inch buffer between our face powder sufficed. (I remember my first air-kiss-gone-wrong, when I planted a good one on a well-known Palm Beach-er. She chuckled. My eyes widened in utter disbelief at my obvious mistake.) Either way, by four o'clock in the afternoon, my event-planning anxiety had dissolved the last of my energy, so I left my favorite donors sipping Earl Grey and escaped to rest for the remainder of the night.

I propped my feet on the couch and scratched across my belly, trying to chase away the tickles. In the silence of my apartment, I tried to nap. But my midmorning indigestion had progressed into a heavy weight against my lungs. The roll of fruit-flavored TUMS refused to calm the pressure.

Then it happened. One gasp followed by strained constriction—as if someone had popped my lung. I banged my fist to my chest to pound out some relief. Nothing. Sitting up straighter, I struggled to suck in air.

"I c-can't breathe—"

My attempts to inhale turned to short breaths, and with each one, my sternum vibrated as if someone were pulling a string of gum-ball-sized pearls through my chest.

I fumbled with the numbers on the phone.

"Hello, 9-1-1; what's your emergency?"

"I-I can barely b-breathe. I-I feel p-pressure on m-my chest . . . There's . . . bumps—"

"Go to the emergency room."

"What?"

"Go to the ER, or I'll send an ambulance. Your choice."

My fingers shook as I dialed my husband's work. Jason made the twenty-minute drive home in ten. I heard the tires skidding on the blacktop seconds before the door flew open. He scooped me up into his faded, black Ford F-150. His confused expression quickly changed to mirror mine: panic.

"You'll be fine . . . Everything will be okay. Breathe slowly." He tugged the shoulder harness across my chest and buckled me in with shaking hands. "We'll be there soon." The car door closed with its usual deafening *bang*.

We cut across town to I-95. But the highway was packed. Of course, it was. We had hit rush hour. The cars surrounding us moved miserably slow. Jason swerved in and out of traffic—as I held my chest, swaying with each jerk—unscathed by Jason's three-inch close calls with neighboring vehicles. For the first time in our marriage, I appreciated his Indy-style maneuvers.

He carried me through the automatic doors at Good Samaritan Medical Center and lowered me onto the seat in front of the dark-haired receptionist. My body slouched forward in an effort to ease the discomfort. I pressed both hands, fingers splayed, across my chest.

"It h-hurts. Wh-what's happening?" I rocked repeatedly now, gasping audibly.

"I'm sorry," Jason said, rubbing my back. "We'll find out soon." His body shook along with the bouncing of his knee. *What's taking so long?*

The dark-haired woman turned and cackled, pushing her coworker's arm, as if she just heard the joke of the day.

Jason interrupted her. "Hey! My wife's in pain! When are you going to call on us?"

The dark-haired lady stiffened.

"I don't have her paperwork." She leaned forward. "Did ya sign in?"

"No." He looked around.

She pointed to the corner. "She needs to sign in with the triage nurse first. Then I register her."

Sign in? Of *course* you have to sign in. I helped raise money for this place; you'd think I'd know that.

With my shoulders hunched and chest curved to ease the pressure, Jason rushed me to the nurse. One mention of my symptoms, and she hollered into a phone. A buzzer sounded, and two large double doors opened. A team helped me onto a gurney and whisked me into the exam room, skipping my appointment with the dark-haired lady.

A swarm of people slapped my now-exposed body with twenty-some stickers with silver nubs and attached wires. I heard snapping noises. Then I felt light pressure along my chest and belly.

"We'll know in a second," I heard a thin blonde mumble to her coworker.

The EKG spit out a report. "It's not her heart!" the blonde yelled.

I tried to suck in more air. My body convulsed. I dug my fingers deeper into the vinyl mattress. "Wh-what is going on? Can you f-feel the vibration in my chest?" I looked at each of them as I wiped tears from my face.

One grabbed my hand and started an IV. Another checked my blood pressure. The third finally turned to face me. "The doctor's on his way, okay?"

The blonde placed her hand on my shoulder. "Are you pregnant?"

"W-we just f-found out. Last week. I'm six w-weeks." I scratched my arm.

"You need a chest X-ray for an accurate diagnosis." The blonde handed me a heavy, gray apron to drape around my waist. "This will shield your abdomen, but you need to sign a release."

I decided to take the risk, signed the papers, and stood against a cold, square plate wearing the twenty-pound lead coat. *Lord, protect my baby.*

"Hold your breath. Don't move," the technician said and stepped out of the room. The machine made a jolting noise. The technician returned and removed the large film from behind me.

"The doctor will see you soon." She rushed out.

Shaking still, I crawled back into bed with Jason's help. He slid beside me, wrapping his arms securely around my hundred-pound body. We rested in silence. Jason kissed my head. Over time, we'd forgotten how to communicate without setting each other off. His arms felt nice, though. Secure even.

Come to think of it, I couldn't remember the last time he had held me so tightly and meant it.

2

WHEN I WOKE, Jason was seated on a plastic chair beside my gurney. I looked at the clock: *6:15. Forty-five minutes. What's taking so long?*

I pushed the tear-dampened hair from my face and forced it behind my ears, certain I had those lovely mascara rings from crying too hard. Then I scratched hard along my jaw, nearly exfoliating the skin with my nails to chase the tickles away.

Lying on the gurney, I switched from hip to hip, searching for a tolerable position and a respite from all the soreness in my upper body. The pressure in my chest now pushed out burps—the embarrassing, openmouthed kind you'd never even want anyone to see. But each release of pent-up air brought a full sixty seconds of comfort. Then, as if on cue, an invisible elephant would again plop, dead center, on my chest. No amount of adjusting, wheezing, or unladylike belching kept him from rebounding.

Blood-pressure cuff on the wall, red biohazard waste box on my right, and canisters on the counter—which I was certain were not filled with lollipops.

I hated where I was.

I had spent five months visiting dermatologists, allergists, and different primary care physicians, but no one could tell me why the underside of my skin itched as if it were infested with fleas. Each appointment had left me with the same hopelessness: it was all in my head, and I had bottles of prescription-strength anti-anxiety pills to prove it. But even at the risk of hearing another doctor label me a hypochondriac, I needed to ask about the itching. Again. I couldn't be making up this chest-pain thing, so maybe the itching was real too.

My eyes closed, and I adjusted my position, rubbing the bottoms of my feet, which now were beaded with sweat as if the pores of my soles were crying along with my body. This wetness was yet another oddity stumping my physicians. I wiped my moistened hands along my gown and tried to focus on minimizing the pain in my chest.

Moments later, the door opened. A tall young man

with black hair entered. I put my hand over my heart and took a shot at a deep breath but failed as soon as the internal bumping rattled inside my sternum.

"Hello, Mrs. Hedegard. I'm Dr. McGarry, the physician on call." He shook my hand. "I'm curious. Have you experienced any other symptoms lately?"

"Y-yes, I have a-anemia, insomnia, f-fatigue."

I tried to calm my gasping before continuing. "I get b-beads of sweat on m-my hands and f-feet, there's pressure on my l-lungs—and a bumping sensation when I b-breathe."

I paused again. "And, I've b-been itching . . . for m-months."

He folded his arms. "There's no easy way to say this. But your symptoms mimic that of a classic case of Hodgkin's lymphoma. You have an eight-inch mass in your chest, about the size of a football. This explains your difficulty breathing and every other irritation you mentioned."

Jason moved closer, and I hung my head into his chest, relieved. "I'm n-not crazy," I whispered.

With a confused expression, Dr. McGarry slowed his speech. "Do you understand what I'm saying? I believe you have cancer."

All I could do was give a quick nod. "Mm-hmm."

Jason pulled me closer. I'm sure he was remembering all the times he had downplayed my complaints about my skin, about wanting to nap all day—even falling asleep at the dinner table from exhaustion—and my sudden phobias of dirt and animal dander. I blamed everything for triggering my irritations.

"I'm sorry. I typically get a different response when I first diagnose patients."

Jason cleared his throat. "She's had more than twenty appointments with doctors. No one could explain her skin problem or, um, the fatigue. They prescribed Xanax for psychosomatic symptoms. Basically, after a slew of negative test results—" Jason rubbed my shoulder— "no one believed her."

"I see. Many miss these symptoms. Your disease is rare. Hodgkin's lymphoma represents less than one percent of all cancer cases in the United States—roughly eighty-five hundred diagnoses a year—and only 25 percent of patients itch. It's common for practitioners to misdiagnose the skin irritation." Dr. McGarry pushed the bridge of his glasses closer to his face. "Had you set foot in my office, I would have recognized the symptoms immediately. But this is my area of expertise."

Fresh tears filled my eyes. "That's so frustrating." My voice broke.

"I understand. Really," he said. "I had Hodgkin's when I was seventeen—a key factor in why I became an oncologist. To save people like us."

I pressed the back of my hand to my mouth and let the tears fall from my face. Everything was finally sinking in.

"Making diagnosis more complicated, your disease affects younger patients ages fifteen to thirty-five, and in some cases, from fifty-five and older."

"But, wh-what causes the itch-ing?"

"No one completely understands what causes it." Dr. McGarry shrugged. "Hodgkin's is a blood-related cancer and runs in the same family as leukemia, except this disease targets the lymph system. One theory is that toxins circulate throughout the lymphatic vessels and nodes, causing discomfort from underneath the skin." He pursed his lips. "I'm deeply sorry."

He rearranged his stance and leaned against the gray counter behind him.

"Fortunately, Hodgkin's is the most curable cancer, especially when treated early. You have a tough choice, though." He tilted his head down. "I'm Catholic. It's against my beliefs to suggest an abortion. But every other doctor in this hospital would recommend terminating your pregnancy followed by aggressive treatment. My guess is . . . you've had this cancer for six months to a year."

I tried to take a deep breath, but the pressure pushed back, and my eyes watered again. "Couldn't y-you just cut th-the tumor out?"

"Good question. But your growth is not one big mass. It consists of tiny pieces of cancer surrounded by scar tissue. It'd be like carving peanut butter out of Jell-O. The consistency of the growth would make it difficult to cut around without endangering surrounding organs. The procedure is risky. You'd be hard pressed to find a surgeon to attempt that type of operation."

"Oh." I rubbed my arm.

"You're a petite girl. What—a little over five feet?"

I nodded.

"You're having trouble breathing now, only six weeks into your pregnancy. My concern is that when your baby grows and pushes against your lungs, with your tiny torso, you're going to have a problem." He squinted. "Do you understand what I'm saying?"

Jason stroked my hand.

I shook my head. "I-I don't think I could d-do that—h-have an abortion."

Jason continued rubbing my skin until it hurt from the repeated motion. His restless leg bounced. "How much time do we have to decide?"

Dr. McGarry sighed. "I'm sorry you're going through this, Mr. and Mrs. Hedegard. You have a lot to think about. Why don't you go home and consider the implications. But I'll need you in my office tomorrow morning with an answer. Your case is complicated and time-sensitive, given the size of your tumor."

He pinched the bottom of his smooth chin with his hand and lowered his voice. "You need to know, though, if you plan to keep the baby, I'll recommend chemotherapy while you're pregnant."

3

As we drove home from the hospital, I felt as if everything good in my life had died. And to be honest, other than raising money for Good Samaritan and St. Mary's Medical Centers to build a children's hospital or a new cancer ward, I had little joy left to begin with.

Our marriage was not filled with cuddling on the front-porch hammock, sipping store-bought iced tea, and giggling while new-romance tingles drifted from head to toe. Yes, this is how I had imagined holy matrimony: an endless lovers' high.

However, when Jason reached over to grab my hand in the passenger's seat, I glanced at our entwined fingers and exhaled more easily, noticing my snuffling and ragged breathing had slowed to a tolerable wheeze.

I hadn't craved his attention this much since college. In fact, the sensation reminded me of the first moment his skin touched mine only five years earlier. . . .

Jason sat beside me while we studied at the distressed picnic table in his college apartment. I had reread the first paragraph of *Beowulf* three times and was debating how to handle my rapid heartbeat. With each accidental graze of his arm against mine, the words jumbled in my brain and slipped away.

It was useless, really, to continue studying.

I considered moving to a different location— unsure why all of a sudden Jason seemed to be more than my English Lit study partner.

He brushed my arm again.

I flinched. My cheeks flushed. I stole a glance at him, then quickly looked back at the page.

"What?" he asked, with a sheepish grin.

"Uh, nothing. I'm—reading—studying, that's all." I played with my pencil, then jumped up. "I think I need to move to the other side of the table." My voice escalated a little.

"I understand." Jason examined me with a crooked smile. "I have that effect on women."

I pushed out a sharp "Ha!" as I stood to move. This quick response tactic, I hoped, would disarm his speculations. And it worked well, I thought, until I tripped over the bench leg.

The words that followed did not help my case. I admitted how his arm brushing mine sent warm tingles along my skin.

From then on, intermittently throughout the evening, Jason leaned in close and asked, "Still feeling hot all over?"

That night I knew I was falling in love with Jason—a boy I'd known only a month. Somehow, God had plunked down, right before my eyes, the hunkiest catch at Palm Beach Atlantic University: a six-foot, blue-eyed blond.

Four months later we were engaged. Four months after that, married.

Our subtle drifting apart, I never saw coming.

We were together but not really. We both worked long hours at various jobs. I waitressed and Jason hopped from wedding photography to cleaning up after rhinos at the zoo. We barely saw each other. And when we *were* together, we fought. About money. About unmet expectations. About everything, it seemed.

The blue NIV *Couples' Devotional Bible* given to us on our wedding day sat bedside, near but untouched. We were six-week church attenders—which meant by week five I had nagged Jason enough that he finally agreed to sit through a service with me. Even though God was the original foundation of our like-mindedness, I really only called on him when I needed something, as if he were my own personal genie. Weekly, I threw a prayer his way.

Lord, help us find better jobs.

Help me get over my cold.

Help me not kill Jason.

The irony of it all was that we had just stumbled on a church that felt like a good fit.

Then illness happened.

I pulled at the ends of my hair. Here we were—driving home from the ER. My mind jumping through the years of college, work, marriage, unmet dreams, pregnancy, cancer.

Jason squeezed my hand. "Everything is going to be okay."

I gave a quick nod. My lip quivered as I wiped my face with my free hand to hide my tears. *Oh, God, we're a mess. And now this.*

Once through the apartment door, I collapsed on our couch, letting the starchy cushions absorb my sobs. Jason followed, stroking my hair. My cries strained my breathing, and the chest-bumping sped up again.

I envisioned the size of the eight-inch mass globbed together in my chest, sitting above my baby. I scrunched my eyes shut and nestled into Jason.

With his arms tight around my body, so comforting, he

promised God would take care of us; then he whispered into my hair, "Let's pray."

Instinctively, Jason and I slid off the couch. For the first time in our marriage, we knelt beside each other and asked God for guidance about my health. The baby. Wisdom for the doctors.

Peace like clouds of hope filled our two-bedroom apartment. Something lifted inside me.

Surreal, supernatural, and rather indescribable—even repeating the incident sounds make-believe. Nonetheless, a weight ascended from my body, my mind, as if someone protected me and the baby. In this serene moment I'm certain I felt God's presence surrounding us.

Then the words popped out. "I'm . . . supposed . . . to keep . . . this baby." I swallowed hard, knowing what this meant.

Jason's eyes met mine. "I know. I felt the same way, but I wanted you to make the decision."

He wrapped his arms around me, engulfing my body. That confirmed it.

I couldn't lie on a table while someone took our child.

4

THE NEXT MORNING I woke with swollen eyes. Pain coursed through my chest with each wheeze.

Bone-weary from the five hours of intermittent rest the insomnia allowed, I rolled into a ball as the events of the last twenty-four hours replayed in my mind. *Oh, God, this can't be happening. You wouldn't allow this to happen.*

Where was the peace I had felt last night?

I stepped onto the elevator heading to the cancer ward. The small space reeked of lemon-scented disinfectant and musty urine. I recoiled, shielding my face. Once the door closed, it was clear that the carpet had been soiled at some point in the last few days. In an effort to mask the stench, the cleaning crew must have fumigated the area with bottles of scented spray. The smells lingered until the doors opened.

We walked toward a brightly lit room where sunbeams streamed from the skylights. *Such a pretty place for so much darkness.* Jason handed my medical information to the young clerk behind the desk. Beside the large fish tank and coffee station to my right, people with weary faces leaned on canes or walkers, and a few sat hunched over their knees.

"Dabney Hedge-a-guard," a gruff-voiced nurse called before we had a chance to sit down. My heart pounded. *Possible life, or death—for me and the baby.* I rested my hand on my belly and let the prayers run through my head: *God, help me. Save me. Heal me.*

At the nurses' station, Jason stood beside me as a rotund woman stuck me twice before hitting a vein. "You've one good vein in your left arm. You'll always need small-gauge butterfly needles—tell your nurses that from now on." She smiled as she withdrew the needle, pressed a cotton ball over the bubble of blood with one finger, and secured it with tape.

"There. Hold the bandage firmly. Don't wanna bruise. Dr. McGarry'll see you in room 2." She pointed across the hall.

I sat on the crisp paper shielding the exam table, and a young nurse handed me a folded disposable gown. "Remove everything up top and put this on, opening in the front."

A few minutes later we heard a tap on the door and Dr. McGarry entered. "Morning," he said. "So. What did we decide?"

Jason and I grabbed hands. "W-we're keeping the baby," I said.

Dr. McGarry rubbed his chin, then shifted his eyes to Jason. "So, what I'm hearing you say is you want me to focus on saving the baby first, and then your wife. That's your decision?"

We nodded.

"All right." Dr. McGarry took a deep breath and let it out. He scanned the chart beside him on the counter. "I'm fairly certain you have Nodular Sclerosing Hodgkin's lymphoma. I'll order a chest core biopsy to sample the mass, a CT scan to get an accurate size of the scarring, and a bone marrow biopsy to confirm your disease hasn't reached your marrow."

My tummy twisted.

Dr. McGarry felt along the sides of my neck, pushing and tapping his fingers as if he were playing the piano. He stopped at my collarbone and slid his fingers sideways, repeatedly touching, examining a raised, painless lymph node above my left clavicle. Round and spongy to the touch, relatively the size of half a globe grape, it protruded a half inch off my neck.

"You have one infected lymph node that I can feel, but the scans will verify if there are more."

My fingers reached my collarbone and memorized the soft, painless form. *How in the world have I never felt this before?*

He moved down under my arms, then poked and massaged a bit above my left hip. "I'm feeling for an enlarged spleen." He pushed to the left of my tummy again. "Does this hurt?"

"No." I looked at Jason, who was seated with his arms crossed, leg bouncing again.

* * *

A few minutes later I sat in another small waiting room. A weathered technician handed me a piece of cloth with strings. "Put this on, opening in back, please."

The temperature in that room had to be fifty degrees. In the dressing room, I put on the gown, gaping holes and all, and wished I had asked for a child's size.

With the gown hanging off my body—nearly touching the floor—I tried to settle myself steadily on the ten-foot-long, slender table. Just then, the air conditioning kicked on. I raised my hand to get her attention. "Do you have a blanket?"

"Sure, hon. I'll be right back." She winked.

With Jason in the waiting area, I had nothing to do but focus on my surroundings. I had held my emotions in all morning. I rubbed my eyes with the palms of my hands. *I'm not going to cry today. Keep it together.* Streams of repetitive prayers started again while the nurse placed a lead shield below my belly button and then draped my body with a warm blanket.

I watched, motionless, as she picked up a syringe from the metal tray behind her and pierced the back of my left hand again and again before capturing a vein.

"I'll push saline first to ensure the IV is working properly, take a couple of scans, and then run iodine as a contrast. It enhances the clarity."

She turned to the silver pole and released a plastic clip. Starting at my wrist, a chilled stream of saline rushed inside my veins along the innermost parts of my arm. Two scans later she said, "Iodine's next. This will create a fiery sensation inside. It's normal. Don't worry, okay, sweetie?" She patted my shoulder and smiled, which caused the creases in her face to deepen.

Like a heating blanket where the coils warm from within, the iodine moved through my capillaries, remedying my chills.

Each time she told me to lie still and hold my breath, which I struggled to do, I thought of the baby, and fresh tears surfaced. *Lord, I want to be done.* I sniffed. *I want to go home.*

* * *

During the bone marrow biopsy, I lay facedown on Dr. McGarry's exam table, dressed in a new gown—this time open in the back. I heard him walk in pushing a cart, instruments clinking from the vibration of unsteady wheels.

He explained this would be the most painful procedure. I held my husband's hand, prepared to squeeze the blood out of each finger when the probing became unbearable. The way Dr. McGarry had described it, I waited for him to hand me a wooden stick to wedge between my teeth to prevent agonizing screams or accidental tongue severing from shock.

He administered a shot of Demerol, a drug similar to morphine, into my backside. A minute later, the heavens opened, and rays of light showered mercy over my body. I melted deeper into the table.

Okay. It was the drugs—but it felt heavenly as each tickle diminished. With all the fatigue, my constant struggle with staying awake now collided with a mystery potion I never knew existed. Lying in a pleasant stupor, I had one thought: *Drugs are a beautiful thing.*

And there I stayed, relishing every second.

"Dabney, I'm starting the procedure now. Here we go."

Dr. McGarry's hand pressed down on the side of my lower back, and I felt pressure from the hollow syringe around my hip bone—nothing else. After five minutes or so I heard him say, "I'm to the marrow; suctioning samples now."

I knew the tests would determine whether the cancer had spread to my bones.

"Dabney, you haven't said much." He chuckled nervously. "Are you okay?"

Indeed I was. So settled in, enjoying the magic of medication for the first time, my thoughts and body rested in peace.

"Dabney, are you in pain?" Dr. McGarry asked again, a little more urgency in his voice.

My lips wouldn't move.

"Dabney, can you hear me?" He talked slowly, loud. "If. You. Are. Okay. Squeeze. Jason's. Hand."

I instructed my muscles to move.

Jason kissed my fingers. "Her fingers flinched."

"Good." I heard Dr. McGarry exhale. "I thought we'd lost you there for a moment. I guess now I can tell you, I've heard grown men howl from this procedure." He gave an awkward chuckle.

I didn't want to wake from my first taste of tranquillity in months. The itching—gone. Breathing—normal. My husband—silent, supporting me. I rested peacefully until my potion wore off.

*   *   *

Thankful my anesthetized hip had stayed numb, I found myself flat on my back on yet another exam table for the chest core biopsy—paper gown open in the front this time. The technician stooped over me and anesthetized between my breasts with a long needle, piercing from place to place.

By the third stick, I no longer felt the stab through my skin, just slight pressure, although I watched the needle lift and lower before my eyes.

"I'm stepping behind the glass." The tech pointed behind him. "I can hear you if you need me. The most important thing to remember is to lie still during the procedure."

I did a quick nod. My chin quavered.

A humming noise started. The needle lowered until it hovered inches from my chest. The first punch startled me. It sounded like an air compressor kicking on. I felt the force and saw the needle snap down again, but I experienced no pain. The needle grabbed sections of the mass with each hit. By the ninth strike, I closed my eyes, praying for the hundredth time that day, as moisture formed on my lids.

I'm only twenty-five.

5

Two weeks after my ER visit I woke without gasping or the weird pearl sensation or pressure on my chest.

Dr. McGarry had thought my breathing would worsen.

After my diagnosis of stage 2A Hodgkin's Nodular Sclerosis, which had an 85 percent cure rate if I started treatment, prayer chains circled the Internet. Strangers e-mailed to say they were praying for a miracle. We all were.

I lifted my hand to my rib cage, continuing to easily breathe in and out.

Normal.

Oh, praise God! I'm healed.

And then I felt them.

Ants, or fleas, or the sensation of sweeps of legs crawled around my body.

I sighed. *I'm still itching.*

6

MID-NOVEMBER 1998

My life felt like a bumper car with a missing steering wheel. My perfectly planned strategy—go to college, get married, become successful in my career, and then have children— had suddenly been derailed by a disease that hit me from behind. Or from the side. It really didn't matter. Cancer was an unwelcomed addition to my life.

My type A personality didn't like this.

The growing uncertainty led to two tactics for dealing with my sickness: prayer—amazing how a tumor got my stagnant relationship with God moving—and research.

Two weeks after my diagnosis, stacks of holistic health

books surrounded me as I sat on the living-room carpet. Each promised to cure the cancer that was feeding off my body. My older sister, Christine, had sent them after I had prattled on and on the week before about a college course I'd taken. The professor had healed himself of prostate cancer through prayer and juicing and visualizing multiple yellow Pac-Man characters devouring his damaged cells. He'd pace in front of his desk, waving an apricot-tinted arm (discolored from his regimen of carrot juice) and proclaiming that sugar hadn't passed his lips in five years.

I remembered thinking that if I ever got sick, I'd save myself that way.

Now, with the mass in my lungs growing each day, I looked at the books strewn across the rug—my only source of control—and felt a trace of hope, thanks to my sister, who always knew how to take care of me.

* * *

Ever since I was five years old, Christine had assumed the role of my mother as we were growing up. She was the one who opened soup cans while Mom worked two and three jobs and crammed in night courses at community college so we could live. Mom did the best she could raising us by herself, and she stubbornly refused to ask Dad for help.

Nonetheless, during my early years, from ages two to seven, my sister's job was to protect me. But when Christine turned thirteen, she fought with Mom one too many times. I have a vague recollection of waking one morning to see my sister staring stone-faced at the front door and gripping a bag in each hand.

"Dad needs her now," Mom said flatly.

That was the last day my sister and I lived together under Mom's roof.

At the age of eight I learned to fend for myself after school until Mom came home at night. I don't remember much of what I ate, or even what I did other than ride my secondhand bike through the neighborhood until the streetlights came on and reminded me to get on home. But I do remember the nights Mom took me dancing at Rosie O'Grady's Good Time Emporium in downtown Orlando. A big, bosomy lady walked the elevated stage through the audience, lashes long and sparkly, the slit in the side of her dress hiked so high that her fancy garter showed. I always wondered if she felt embarrassed. But then she'd throw back her head and belt out some bluesy number. Mom and I danced in the aisle while the men at the bar clapped and handed me bottomless Shirley Temples. They handed Mom glasses of something else.

Those were my best memories with Mom before she sent me to live with Dad when I was ten. He lived the next state away, in Atlanta, and fought a losing battle to stay sober. During that short, six months away, I sure missed Mom and her outlandish love of life. I even mailed her pennies and nickels, all the change I could gather, to see if my scrapings would help her move me back home. It wasn't that Dad was mean or boring, it was just hard smelling the vodka and orange juice or hearing his slurred sentences as he tried desperately to communicate with the daughter he loved and, I assumed, wanted to connect with. I loved the gold necklace he bought me, and I learned to like the gourmet meals he prepared every night—except for all the vegetables. He tried, but alcohol had ensnared his mind so much that he couldn't break away on his own.

We would find out later, around the time I enrolled in college, when our relationship had grown stronger, that Dad had ingested so much alcohol his kidneys started giving him problems. Type 2 diabetes had set in, and doctors warned that his health was in jeopardy. At that point, Dad met a Christian woman who refused to date him until he was sober. He rushed to an AA meeting, and he eventually beat his addiction, married the woman who became my stepmom, and turned his life over to the Lord. I had no idea then that in my adulthood we'd become the closest of friends.

During that six-month separation from Mom, I learned she was selling our furniture to pay the bills, all the while juggling her nighttime habits. One day her landlord stopped taking lamps and fans as payment and offered her free rent if she'd attend a Sunday service with him.

When Mom showed up at Dad's door to move me back

to Florida, all I could think was that maybe my piggy-bank contributions really had helped get her back on her feet. But she beamed with a different kind of look in her eye on that long drive home. "The church saved me from myself," was all she cared to explain.

I believed her.

Once back in Orlando, Mom's usual overnight guests no longer showed up, her unpredictable moods leveled out, and the smile on her face radiated from within, not from what she had ingested.

Whatever had changed Mom, I needed for myself. I bet that landlord never knew his offer to miss a few bucks for a month or two changed the course of our lives forever. His church introduced me to Jesus—my new refuge.

* * *

I shook my head at the distant memories and picked up my first book on how to beat cancer.

In a few hours' time, the paperback was dog-eared and underlined. I sensed control shifting back to me as what I read unlocked medical mysteries, even, purportedly, uncovering the cause of my disease: environmental toxins and excessive stress.

I read how my fruits and vegetables were wrapped in pesticides, my meat laden with growth hormones and antibiotics. How detergents, fertilizers, and other hazardous material percolated through the soil and the water table and eventually from my faucet into my glass. Fats, dairy products, salt, high-fructose corn syrup, sugar, white flour, and processed foods all bombarded my system. Add to that the unnatural substances surrounding me and seeping through my skin and, ultimately, into my blood—from pollution, radiation, synthetic fibers, cosmetics, and scented lotions—and, so the book said, my compromised immune system didn't stand a chance.

But the chapter I read and reread claimed cancer patients could calculate a year or two prior to their diagnosis and pinpoint towering amounts of stress—say a divorce, the loss of a loved one, or a nervous breakdown. According to the book, anxiety weakens the immune system, which leaves the body in the most fragile of states and opens the door for irregular cells to mutate and reproduce, thus birthing cancer cells.

In essence, the book claimed, worry welcomed disease.

My thoughts raced as I tried to dissect every stressor I was aware of in the previous two years of my life.

Marriage? No. Jason and I had fought since day one.

Money? We had never had enough to begin with.

I scratched my scalp to relieve the itching.

A traumatic event? *Think. Was anything causing me to cry, obsess? . . . Any traumatic event?*

Oh.

I sat up straight. *Bingo!*

* * *

I can see my boss clearly. Sitting behind the dented metal desk, papers neatly stacked—in some sort of methodical order, I'm sure—asking me about simple errors, errors my brain couldn't catch. Donors from our nonprofit agency were calling, my employer said, questioning a recent fundraising letter I had mailed to thousands of supporters, thanking them for "helping us to raise over $17,00!"

"What is 'one-seven-comma-zero-zero'?" I was asked during our private meeting.

Obviously I had left off the third zero. I internally kicked myself.

The office was cold. I saw my boss's lips moving, but all I heard was an accusing voice inside me: *Idiot. Where did you graduate from? Incompetent blonde!* That's not what anyone said—but I believed that's what my boss thought.

And with that, my childhood secret was out. My struggle with dyslexia had haunted every paper I touched in school. I couldn't spell, and I couldn't remember those ridiculous grammar rules.

With a wounded heart—or maybe it was a wounded ego—I apologized. As I walked down the scuffed-up hallway to my desk, I kept repeating the word *probation . . . probation . . . probation.*

Although I'd never been in trouble at work before, my

boss now wanted to see every letter I wrote before it left the office. But my best writing attempts landed back on my desk, scribbled with screaming red corrections.

With each marked-up paper, the pain of my childhood struggles in school resurfaced, and I relived the shame of failing fourth grade while living with Dad in Atlanta. It wasn't his fault I could barely read. Or comprehend. Or untangle the letters that reversed so easily in my mind. No one had ever addressed the issue before.

Each day at the office, I completed my work at record speed, but by bedtime I lay in a ball crying, my brain utterly spent from rehearsing my latest mistakes. My gut knotted tight, and I squeezed my knees to my chest and tried to control my sobs so Jason wouldn't feel them.

I lost weight and sleep and worked through most lunches. My neck stiffened each time I heard my boss walking down the hall. I wanted to please my employer, to hear compliments on a job well done. But my best efforts were always met by red-lined memos. After a few more weeks, emotionally exhausted and almost devoid of self-confidence, I quit.

I quickly found a new job as assistant director of development at Intracoastal Health Foundation, which benefited two of the largest hospitals in Palm Beach County. With it came an eight-thousand-dollar raise and my first smile in months.

This was my clean break. A chance to start over.

I hugged coworkers, even my boss, and exited through the glass doors. The constriction in my throat relaxed with each step to my car.

* * *

I lowered the book to the floor, calculating all the various factors. My mental breakdown had occurred a year and half earlier.

I'm my own worst enemy. I've poisoned myself with sense-less worrying.

7

DECEMBER 1, 1998—JOURNAL ENTRY

"I am tired, pale, weak. I have no energy. I want to be happy—I want to smile and laugh. I don't want to cry anymore. . . . I would do anything to have just one normal day again. . . . I wake up sometimes in the middle of the night with a sharp pain in my chest. I am so scared. Please help me, God!"

* * *

A month into my self-imposed diet of homemade distilled water, organic beans, fruits, vegetables, and daily juicing of carrots and apples, I still felt crummy. And I'd lost more than a few pounds.

I cooked with glass or metal and practically tethered our new air-filtration system to my leg as I moved from room to room, trying to rid my apartment of the nasty toxins the books suggested were surrounding me.

God, I don't want to go through chemo and radiation. Am I playing with my life? I lowered my head. *I have to—for the baby, I'll do anything.*

MID-DECEMBER 1998

In Mom's efforts to help, she tracked down a pricey herb that promised to destroy cancer cells, warts, moles, and a crazy list of other ailments.

Intrigued, I applied the paste each morning to a brown growth on my left leg below my hip. By day seven, the mole had shriveled to a pale, spongy nub and dropped off with the swipe of a tissue. I stared at the remaining pockmark. It worked. Following the recommendations on the jar, I added a half teaspoon of the paste to my organic orange juice as my morning tonic. But even with all my experimenting, my itching intensified.

I made it to my second trimester frail, drained, and bony.

"Whatever you're doing, you need to stop," Dr. McGarry said. "Treatment brings on unpleasant side effects. Not being able to keep food down is one of them. You need to get your weight back up before you start chemotherapy. Please, eat a steak; eat *something*. Just put weight on. The baby needs it just as much as you do."

He continued his lecture, but I didn't listen. I imagined how God would heal me through living a healthier life. I was helping my cells the only way I knew how.

Suppressing my scratching, I nodded along as Dr. McGarry continued his speech. My self-induced weight loss concerned him, but the fact that my tumor wasn't affecting my breathing and the absence of any new symptoms such as night sweats or an enlarged spleen meant he would postpone treatment until something changed.

Over the course of the next couple of weeks, my dependency on alternative sources of treatment increased. I added a special cleansing tea, a secret jungle juice, and a powder that claimed to rebuild and strengthen the genetic makeup of every cell. I even hooked myself to a machine that promised to shock the parasites that could be consuming my body. Every brochure I read promised miraculous results. Add in all the extra prayers I voiced throughout my day, and I felt sure God would heal me.

No one needed to know the extent of my dabbling. This was between God and me.

8

Sitting at my desk, I propped my head on my hand to read the *Palm Beach Daily News* society section, researching the coverage of local fund-raising galas. When I woke, my elbow bent sideways and barely supporting my face, I decided to end the day early to catch up on last-minute Christmas shopping at a discount department store.

It took little time to make my selection: green-and-white polka-dotted boxers for Jason and an ivory crewneck sweater for my father-in-law.

As I bent over the counter to write my check, chills moved across my body.

My penmanship looked scribbly, as if I were writing while driving over pebbles. I tried to steady my hand, but the odd sensation intensified.

Then my legs, already feeling rubbery, decided they could no longer do their job of supporting me.

As I began to stammer, "I'm about to faint—" my pen dropped from my hand and clattered on the Formica counter. My world went black.

I awoke wondering why my head was cushioned in a red-haired lady's lap. My eyes darted around the many faces streaked with concern and staring at me. With the bright fluorescent lights glaring above me, I squinted as a clerk handed me a plastic cup. "Drink this."

The redhead lifted me higher, making it easier to swallow.

"Girl, you gave us a scare. How you feelin'?" my cup-bearer asked.

I sipped. "Okay." The cup trembled in my hand. I tried to remember something—anything—about why this overly friendly stranger was cradling my back.

"The ambulance is almost—"

Shopping. That's right. I couldn't believe I was sprawled on the floor. *Great! Everyone's staring.*

I rummaged through my purse and pulled out a box of organic raisins. I chewed while explaining my medical history, only to hear a loud, determined voice behind me say, "Move to the side, please!"

To my horror, three young EMTs hustled through the door, their blue uniforms taut against their arms and chests. Two carried a stretcher, the third, a big red box.

My mouth opened a little as I watched the crowd grow larger.

Oh, Lord, help me now, I prayed silently.

One EMT placed a cuff on my left arm, which, of course, caused the itchies to congregate under the synthetic fabric. I was told not to move. Another pulled a stethoscope from his box, and the third one asked, "Do you have any medical conditions we need to be aware of, ma'am?"

My eyes shifted to the specks in the terrazzo floor. I gave the quick version. He lifted my waif-like wrist to check my pulse.

"I'm fine. Really. My blood sugar must have dropped. I just need something to eat," I said, trying but no doubt failing to appear normal like the rest of the sane people standing around.

"Either way, ma'am, we have to take you to the hospital, especially given your condition."

"I'm fine. I promise. I work for the hospital. . . . I feel better now. I just need to get home." My free arm crossed over my barely-there belly as I pleaded with God that this man would let me go.

"We can't let you drive, ma'am. We can only release you if someone takes you to the ER for a full evaluation."

I called my boss to drive me back to work.

Ten minutes later, we exited through Marshalls's automatic doors and walked past the ambulance and fire truck parked lopsidedly on the curb.

9

Paper-lined exam table, dimly lit room, and Jason standing beside me for my four-month prenatal visit meant one thing: the big reveal of the baby's gender. I weighed in at a hundred and one. Nine pounds lighter than my pre-pregnancy weight.

My OB was not happy.

She questioned the bones protruding from my shoulders. I confessed my new veggie diet and pulled out my baggie of organic carrots, hoping the sight of me gnawing away on them would appease her.

It didn't. I put my snacks away.

When the tech slopped a glob of blue gel on my belly and rolled around the cold wand, I grabbed Jason's hand. I tried hard not to scratch across the sticky mess and interfere with her exam.

"Everything's right on target." She slid the wand to the left side of my belly. "Interested in knowing what you're having?"

We nodded.

"Girl."

I squeezed Jason's hand. "Girl? We're having a girl." My eyes watered, and a bigger than usual smile spread across my face.

Jason couldn't stop wiping his eyes.

I chuckled. "You're so emotional. What guy cries during an ultrasound?"

"One that's sensitive. A quality most people find endearing." He cleared his throat.

Our daughter moved around the screen. *Is she sucking her thumb?* I wondered. *Oh, Lord, please. I can't go through chemo while I'm pregnant.* My nose and the backs of my eyes burned from tears that suddenly surfaced. *God, heal me.* I leaned my head back on the stiff bed. *Please.*

I wiped my cheeks.

I left the appointment with my small portfolio of black-and-white alien images. My favorite captured an arrow pointing to what looked like a miniature hot dog bun. How they knew that's what made her a girl was a mystery to me.

On the ride home I traced the outline of the tiny profile with my finger.

Barely able to function from fatigue and noticeably hungry most of the time, I questioned how my wonder diet might affect her. If I didn't gain weight, maybe she wouldn't either. After reading so many differing health theories, I hated the uncertainty I felt about what was right or wrong to eat.

At eleven that morning I caved in and indulged in a big, fat hamburger. With each bite, my guilty conscience harassed me.

I give up. All this worrying has to be more damaging than what food I eat. Lord, protect me. Protect her. I have to stop evaluating everything that enters my mouth, or I'll go crazy.

When I arrived at work, I used my outdoor voice to announce I was having a girl. The offices three doors away must have heard me.

I sat at my desk, admiring the view of downtown West Palm Beach through my floor-to-ceiling glass wall and patted my minibump. All the while, my thoughts of fatty meat bothered me so much so that I searched the Internet for Bible verses about food.

Romans 14:6-7 from *The Message* reads, "What's important in all this is that if you keep a holy day, keep it for *God's* sake; if you eat meat, eat it to the glory of God and thank God for prime rib; if you're a vegetarian, eat vegetables to the glory of God and thank God for broccoli. None of us are permitted to insist on our own way in these matters."

I sat back in my chair with a sigh. *Meat is mentioned in the Bible. It can't be too awful for me then, right?* I scratched my right arm, unaware of my reactive response to the tingles until I felt a sharp sting above my wrist. Moisture gathered under my nails, and I looked down to see blood dribbling along my forearm from a new, two-inch-long flesh wound.

I gritted my teeth, shook my head.

Make the itching go away. Please, God! I leaned my head back into my chair and squeezed my eyes closed. *Don't cry. Don't cry. I'm having a girl. God is in control. Jason's being supportive for a change.*

But the burning and throbbing made me want to pull off my flesh.

Lord, I want to be done. But the longer I wait to start chemo, the healthier the baby will be.

I'm enduring this for her.

10

ONCOLOGY VISITS, high-risk-pregnancy screenings, CT scans, bimonthly ultrasounds, blood work, and simply walking through a hospital door—where it seemed they charged for each step—added up to one big financial avalanche.

We secretly hoped the bill fairy would wave her magic wand and make the mushroomed stack of overdue statements disappear. She didn't. This only increased the tension between Jason and me.

With fear—the enemy of my soul—sitting smack-dab on my shoulder, swinging its legs and whispering doubts into my ear, it was easy for me to hide and mope about the horribleness of what I was going through—and why it had happened to me.

I was a good person, doing good work raising money for charitable causes, including finding a cure for the very disease that was taking over my body.

In times of peace, when Jason and I talked and loved and laughed, I latched on to him, sucking life from his faith-filled, optimistic view and draining happiness from him until my security tank had filled and I plopped off like a fattened tick, content to live a few more days before again seeking his reassurance.

His "You wait. God will show up in a mighty way" speech always did the trick.

But when his words faded, my simplistic views returned. I wanted our pre-sickness, ignorant bliss back: those nights filled with stupid fights about the fifty bucks he spent on clothes from Gap without asking.

I used to hate him for that.

Now I found myself secretly coping with the miserable state of my body. Doing things I never wanted anyone to know.

Some nights I sat on the bed, leg propped across my knee, dragging the tip of the scissors gently along the insole of my foot, back and forth, back and forth, ever so slightly, until the pain pulled my attention away from the tingles underneath my skin. The slow raking across my skin was glorious, and I no longer cared that the bottom of my foot throbbed and had turned rosy red.

The itching crawled inside my ears. In my nose. Along my tongue. Under the thin skin between my toes. But when scabs appeared along my body from all the skin tearing, I reminded myself, *God will heal me.* I'd hold my head in my hands. *I'm not going through treatment. I'm doing this for the baby. God, help me. God, help me. God, help me.*

But to be honest, even with the growth in my prayer life, I didn't feel as close to God as I once had. Not like in college, when I attended chapel twice a week. Or when I was surrounded by girlfriends reading through our *Experiencing God* devotional.

Or the first time I audibly heard his voice . . .

* * *

Two months into our relationship, Jason and I took a road trip to visit my sister, Christine, in Atlanta.

Christine's approval meant the world to me. Dad was happy because I was happy, and Mom had already offered Jason a ladder to my bedroom window and a thousand bucks for us if we eloped. Mom said she knew the second she shook Jason's hand that he was the man she'd been on her knees praying for. So when Christine laughed along with his jokes and enjoyed his intellectual side, I finally relaxed, and the lump in my throat dissolved.

While we were in Atlanta, my eccentric side, the one

that enjoyed rummaging through secondhand stores for grunge, goth, or basically any funky clothing, surfaced. Lucky for me, Atlanta had a trendy shopping area called Little 5 Points which had indie-style stores. Jason and I dug through the mismatched outfits—everything from odd to zany—at the Junkman's Daughter and Psycho Sisters, looking for secondhand dresses. After an hour, I had settled on a wood-handled patchwork purse.

We continued walking along Euclid Avenue until we stopped in front of Stefan's Vintage Clothing Store. Mannequins displayed timeless fashions that matched perfectly with the dainty heels sitting along the red velour fabric of the window display.

I pulled Jason inside. We fingered through silk, velvet, fringe, furs, gowns, plaid vests, and pinstriped suits. Fedoras and cloches and 1950s gauntlet gloves hung from the tops of the circular clothing wheels. I smiled as I took in all the elegance, imagining how romantic living in that bygone era would have been.

Then I stopped short.

A wall of vintage wedding dresses lined the back of the shop. White lace, miniature pearls, open backs; I admired their beauty, examined the delicacy of the handmade fabrics. But one in particular caught my attention. I pulled it off the rack.

"If that dress fits you," I heard a raspy voice say, "I'll take twenty-five bucks off."

I opened the dress in search of the size.

"Can't tell you how many brides-to-be attempt to wiggle into that gown. It never fits." The attendant waved her hand away, then coughed. "Rib section's slender, and the bodice—it's too short."

"Try it on," Jason said.

I held the dress higher, turning it from back to front, examining the lace train. "Really?" I looked back at him, gave an awkward chuckle.

"Sure. Why not? What could it hurt?"

I stepped into a curtain-lined dressing room. Just then, a black velvet dress flew over the top of the metal pole supporting the makeshift fitting room. Jason's hand grasped the hanger. "Try this, too."

I climbed into the black dress with a raw-silk neckline first. I twirled in front of the mirror and watched, in love with such an elegant piece of cloth, as the short skirt floated over my body. I swished open the curtain.

Jason smiled. "Nice. Fits perfect."

Jason spun me into his arms for a kiss. "Try the other gown," he said, his eyes locked on mine.

My eyes widened, and I reentered the dressing room. Once I had slipped through the lacy material, the gown hung close to my body and followed every curve; it even accommodated my short waist and petite legs. The only alteration needed was a one-inch shortening in the sleeves.

I opened the curtain. Jason's face changed with a growing grin. "We'll take it."

"What? Are you serious?" I whispered. "We're not even engaged!"

"Not yet." He winked at me and turned to the clerk. "She wants the black velvet dress, too. How much for both?"

"One-thirty-five. I can't believe that gown fits her. That dress has been here for years. Looks like it's been waiting for her."

We walked out of the store into the cool Georgia air. I stopped. My stomach turned uneasily as I stared at the pavement, unsure which direction to walk next. Or what to say to this man I'd known for only sixty days. And yet a garment bag draped over my arms held the most important article of clothing I'd ever wear, signifying something greater than either of us had admitted to each other.

Jason lifted the bag, slung the gowns to one shoulder, then slipped his fingers through mine.

"There's no need to worry." He faced me. "You knew we were heading in this direction. Trust me." He squeezed my hand and kissed my cheek. "God's got big plans for us."

When I arrived back at my dorm a week later, I confided to Stephanie, one of my suite mates, about the crazy purchase Jason and I had made.

She beamed, yet all the while, I questioned. "What am I doing? I don't really know him. I mean, he seems like everything I've prayed for in a husband. He even fits the journal description I wrote out in high school. How funny is that?" I chuckled. "But this is moving fast, you know?"

"Pray about it. Ask God. He'll make it clear if this is the man he's called you to marry," Stephanie said, then giggled. She was always so joy filled. That was the biggest difference between us. I worried. She worshiped. Boy, I wished I had more of her faith-filled spirit.

That night I stepped out onto our balcony with my *Experiencing God* devotional and Bible, sat cross-legged with my back against the cement wall, and prayed. *Lord, I need to know if Jason's the one. This is huge.* Huge. *Please give me a sign. A big neon one above his head would be awesome—but I'm thinking that's not going to happen. I need some sort of clue. I don't want to make a mistake. I love him—I think. It's all happening so fast.*

I started to write: "1-10-95: Dear God—if it is meant for Jay & me to be as serious as we are—" Then I heard them. There was no mistaking it. My hand couldn't keep up with the words flying through my head. I wrote, "—please show me by having Jay give me a yellow flower—if he doesn't give me one, then I will know that we are not ready yet. Thank you, God."

Yellow flower? Isn't that a friendship flower? That can't be right. I thought of scratching that part out, certain I had heard God wrong. But I couldn't. I prayed again. *Okay, God. I'm trusting you. This is crazy! But I need to know this is the man you picked for me.* Nine days later, Jason phoned and said he had a surprise for me. "Wear your black velvet dress tonight. I'll pick you up at seven."

I walked out of Johnson Hall and met Jason with a kiss.

From behind his back, he pulled a bouquet. White daisies, purple crocuses with orange stamens, and sprinkled throughout—yellow gerbera daisies.

My hands flew to my mouth and I gasped as tears filled my eyes.

"You're crying?" Jason said. "You . . . don't like them." He pulled back with a confused look. "I should've gotten roses. They're so predictable, though."

"No. It's not that at all. I just, I prayed—" I blinked away the moisture— "and asked God for a sign. If I was supposed to . . . If we were supposed to—you know—get married. And . . . I felt like he said you would give me yellow flowers." I sighed, looking at them. "I know, stupid, right?" Then I started backpedaling. "I mean, I thought it was stupid, because yellow is a friendship flower. I questioned God. How silly is that?"

Jason wiped my face. "Not silly at all. To tell you the truth, I started with a bouquet of pure white daises—like you. Perfect. I started to walk out of the shop, but stopped at the door. I asked the clerk to add a little color. Maybe some purple and yellow."

I waved my hand in front of my face and let out a breath. More tears fell; I leaned into his shoulder.

"These are happy tears, right?"

I nodded into his chest and let out a little laugh. "Of course they are. This means—" I sniffed again— "you're going to be stuck with me for a long time."

Jason surprised me with a Star Line Fun Cruise for their "Shrimp Boat Night" along the Intracoastal Waterway. When the boat docked again at nine thirty, he drove me along North County Road on Palm Beach. We ended the night parked down Casa Bendita Street, where he pulled up in front of a white, Regency-style mansion only a block from the Atlantic Ocean.

Fingers entwined, we walked to an intimate, coquina-rock gazebo, manicured with shrubs. The salty cool air swirled around us. From his pocket he pulled a sheet of well-worn paper and read a poem about a faceless, blonde angel from his dreams. The day he met me, he said, the face became clear.

I wiped my eyes as he knelt to propose.

I threw my arms around him. "Yes!"

We stayed at ground level until sirens startled us.

In the blinding, flashing blue lights, we raised our hands.

"You're on private property," the officer barked.

"Mrs. Shuster won't be happy to know you're badgering her guests, sir," Jason said.

"Huh. That's funny. Mrs. Shuster called us, saying a couple of kids were trespassing." He dropped his light, and I blinked through the floating spots in my eyes.

Jason glanced at me. "I visited her earlier this week, asked permission to use her gazebo to propose. She has a copy of my license." Jason pulled his wallet from his pants pocket.

That's when the officer told us he received calls weekly from Mrs. Shuster, complaining that someone was robbing her. Apparently, her memory wasn't so sharp. "I'll smooth things over. But you'll have to clear out," he said, as he started walking back up the pebbled path. "Just curious," he said, turning back. "Did she say yes?"

"Of course, sir." Jason held out his hands as if to say, "Why wouldn't she?"

Later that night, back in my dorm, I taped two yellow flowers in my journal next to the wedding dress tag and store receipt, and then wrote, "Thank you, God, for answering my prayer—on Jan 19, 1995—Jay gave me 15 daisies w/ about 6 yellow flowers stuck in—and then he asked me to marry him! Thank you, God!"

11

So NAIVE. So in love. So close to God.

But now, much had changed. It was amazing to think how far back I'd slid spiritually.

In the early years of our marriage, the only time I sensed God's presence was when I shifted uncomfortably in the seat at church because I knew God was calling me back to him. Of course, Jason and I struggled to agree on denomination and music style and what the outside of God's building should look like—important matters of the heart.

I assumed we'd be Baptists.

I'd often heard people say, "Baptist born, Baptist bred, and when I die, I'll be Baptist dead." Well, I wasn't born into the denomination, but Mom and Ernie, my step-dad since I was ten, more than made up for lost time by practically making church my second home. We attended Sunday morning, Sunday night, and Wednesday evening. And I learned some of my first Bible songs sitting cross-legged after school while my King's Kids daycare teacher strummed her tan guitar. I loved hymns and that Southern Baptist preaching style and watching the visiting revival pastors redden when they spoke profoundly from the pulpit.

Devoted to the church and to God and serving Wednesday-night spaghetti dinners was the way I envisioned raising my family—especially since I credited my youth pastor for saving me from repeating unhealthy patterns. Brother Mike often challenged us teens, "If you're on a date and wonder what you should or shouldn't be doing, carry a quarter in your pocket." He paused for effect. "If you're too afraid to call me and ask, then you probably shouldn't be doing it."

His implied threat kept me from sliding too deeply into trouble during my high school years, partly because I repeated his quarter question during iffy encounters, sometimes listening, sometimes not. And partly because our town was so small that if anything scandalous went down at the Dizzy Peacock Deli and gas station after hours, most everyone knew about it the next day.

Even Brother Mike.

This I found out the hard way, because the first time my close friend Jennifer and I skipped the bus in seventh grade to walk to school—which made my tummy a little queasy—five people called Mom. "Dabney and Jennifer just walked past my hair salon (flower shop, diner, law office) and are headed down Main Street at nine o'clock. What's your daughter up to?"

Word spread like a pitcher of spilled sweet tea. Inevitably, the youth group heard more lessons on accountability the following week.

Kids needed that kind of liability, I always thought. Church was the perfect place to get it. Jason, on the other hand, hopped from Lutheran to Presbyterian to whatever corner chapel his parents stumbled upon, because during his childhood, they moved more than twenty times up and down the east coast from Maine to Florida. They even lived at a mission in New Jersey, where Jason's dad, a biology and theology graduate, preached from time to time while his mom, a pediatric nurse, helped prepare cafeteria meals.

Somehow, even with a part-time preaching father, Jason's idea of attending church was more like getting a tune-up every couple of months.

That would never fly in my hometown. The pastor would have been at his front door to see if he needed prayer. Or a meal. Or rededication.

After repeated Saturday-evening debates on how to spend our Sunday mornings, Jason and I finally agreed on sampling local services to see who could entertain us the best.

Our first stop: a local Southern Baptist service.

As we walked hand in hand through the door, a white-haired man with thick, wrinkly skin welcomed Jason with a bulletin and bright smile. He slowly bent to my eye level. "Wait one minute there, young lady. I've got a treat *just* for you." He shuffled to the side and grabbed something from the table behind him.

I prepared myself to be decorated with a pretty yellow, embroidered flower decal my home church used for new attendees. This let everyone know who the visitors were so we would be extra friendly to them. Or maybe this was "Ladies Appreciation Day," and I'd receive a delicate rose.

I smiled in anticipation—until he presented me with a Jesus coloring book complete with a packet of crayons.

My smile faded as the old man patted my head as if I were a puppy.

I spun around, twirling my floral empire-waist dress, and yanked Jason up the stairs to the balcony, where I clipped the edge of the first pew. I sulked while everyone else sang "How Great Thou Art." Jason's laughter shook the bench, and I just knew the whole row was focused more on us than on that minister. I silently sobbed, wiping my cheeks with the palms of my hands.

Although the pastor preached the way I liked, I brooded about returning, fearing others had witnessed the little mix-up. I got the "You shouldn't worry so much about what others think" speech on the ride home. I knew it wasn't the elderly man's fault that my round face and petite frame made me look twelve. Sad to say, my embarrassment over that episode kept me from returning to the kind of church I had loved most.

A nondenominational church in Jupiter occupied our attention sporadically for the next several months. We fell in love with the preacher's topical teaching and his charismatic style. Then one Sunday he admitted he'd been sleeping with a woman who was not his wife and he would step down from the ministry to work on restoring his marriage and his relationship with God. I sat in shock and saddened that something like this could happen to such a powerful preacher.

We continued our search. Next we visited Calvary Church in Jupiter, which had a congregation of fifty and met in a high school auditorium, not in a beautiful build-ing with stained-glass windows. The contemporary, U2-esque music lifted my spirit, something I never expected, because they weren't singing hymns. When the pastor interwove biblical teachings from the original Greek and Hebrew and taught the whole chapter of Matthew 17, I was stunned to learn that some Bible scholars believe many of Jesus' disciples were teenagers. I had always envisioned the disciples with beards and hairy chests and the wisdom that came with age.

Later I told Jason, "I learned more in that one sermon than I have in my whole adult life in church."

The summer of 1998 we started attending Calvary off and on, and after a few months, we even joined a marriage Bible study group. I finally felt things could change now that we had church on our side. Within a couple of months, new friendships emerged in response to a single phone call: "Dabney's six weeks pregnant and has an eight-inch-wide, three-inch-thick tumor in her chest."

The prayer chain spread the request from friends to strangers.

Once news of my disease rippled through the growing congregation, our new church family left so many prayer messages on our phone that we no longer picked up. Overwhelmed by support, we were simply too exhausted to keep repeating the story. People kindly dropped off meals, sent care packages, and anonymously mailed cards with cashier's checks tucked inside. All the while, I lay on the couch for hours, curled underneath a blanket, mentally and physically spent.

Then an odd thing happened.

Within one week, two couples from our marriage group asked if we'd like to move in with them, rent free, since God had put our situation so strongly on their hearts.

By the time the second offer was presented, Jason and

I grabbed hands underneath the restaurant table and did a double squeeze.

Not wanting to ruin any friendships even before they started, and realizing that the logical choice was space and location, we accepted Brett and Colleen's offer. They had recently purchased a two-story home located the shortest distance from our work.

"We'll save seven hundred dollars a month to put toward bills and a down payment for a house!" I jumped up and down in our living room full of half-packed boxes, waving my perfectly calculated budget.

"You think?" Jason said teasingly.

"Whatever. You know the way my mind works. I'm a planner." I shrugged. "This fits nicely into my color-coded spreadsheet. God sure did show up."

12

IT WAS MIDNIGHT by the time Jason and I decided to agree to disagree on a silly subject. We'd been living with Brett and Colleen for only two months when the added stress in our lives further strained our marriage.

With my hands full of a sleeping bag, blankets, and pillows, I huffed to the sunroom and arranged a new pallet on the carpet. Wrapping my pillow around my head, I maneuvered myself so I was facing the sliding glass doors that overlooked the pool.

I stared at the stars and shivered and cried until my heart felt swollen from the pressure.

The next morning, after I got up and showered, I walked up to Jason and leaned into him with my arms wrapped around his belly. I pressed my head into his chest as a peace offering.

He gave my back a pat and then disentangled my arms. I couldn't muster an apology, and the fact that we were standing in someone else's kitchen with other people around magnified the awkwardness.

I rushed off to work unsettled in my spirit.

God, I want to be normal. Why aren't you healing me? I'm broken, we're fighting . . . miserable. To top it off, itching all over for nine months is the closest thing to hell I can imagine. I hate my life.

My eyes watered at the thought that popped into my head: *Would anyone care if I were gone?*

On the sidewalk below my fourth-floor office window, healthy people walked the streets, ate sack lunches, and skated along the waterway. But the voice in my head— the one I tried to ignore—repeated the question: *Would it really matter if I were gone?*

I bit my lip, trying to ignore the sensation of fleas biting the backs of my thighs. *I'm not scratching.*

I looked at the window again. *Just jump,* the voice in my head whispered.

Who was I kidding? I'd mess that up, too.

My office door opened, and I heard the receptionist say, "You got a package."

I quickly rubbed my hands down my legs, plastered a grin on my face, and swiveled my chair to face her. "Thank you."

I opened the brown package and pulled out a decorated paper box filled with Hershey's Kisses. The foil-wrapped chocolates covered all but a corner of a note that read "Kiss your worries good-bye! Use this box to throw away your troubles. Love, Christine."

Tears, too many to count, fell and soaked my paper desk calendar.

I loved my sister. And I loved my husband—at least every other day. His confidence—I sighed. That's what had attracted me to him, what I specifically prayed for in a husband.

I patted my growing belly and thanked God. They *would* care if I were gone.

Scribbling my first worry on a scrap of paper, I deposited it in the box and enjoyed my chocolaty treat. Sugar, *mmm*. I hadn't eaten any in months.

A little can't hurt. I leaned back in my chair. *I've already surrendered to red meat. Everything in moderation. Thanks, Sis. You may never know it, but your gift saved me today.*

I grabbed my pen and wrote down all the worries bombarding me:

- "I am worried that I'll be too sick to carry my baby to term."
- "I am worried that my cancer is growing and I will not be able to breathe."
- "I am worried that I am not doing enough at work."

- "I am worried that if I wait too long to get treatment, they will not be able to cure me."
- "I am worried that I have already harmed my baby."
- "I am worried that I will never stop itching."
- "I am worried about what to eat and what not to eat."
- "I am worried that we won't be able to find a good house in a good neighborhood for the price we want."
- "I am worried that labor will be too difficult and will hurt too much."
- "I am worried that my baby will have a developmental disability."
- "I am worried that we don't have a down payment for a house."
- "I am worried about who will watch my baby when I go back to work."

Before I could write my last thought, my phone rang. Apologies rushed out as Jason and I asked for a do-over. He couldn't focus at work, he said. He missed me, loved me, and wanted to work on communicating better.

Thank you, God.

A funny thing happened, though. I found that relying on something simple like a prayer box helped put my worries behind me.

Who knew that one day my sister would go on to market these prayer boxes from her basement and share my story on the card? Or that hundreds of people would pass on this boxed gift to loved ones who were begging God for a miracle? Or that strangers would one day send me encouraging e-mails or handwritten notes to tell me that they were praying for me, for the baby?

I reread the Scripture verses taped to my monitor: "We also rejoice in our sufferings, because we know that suffering produces perseverance; perseverance, character; and character, hope" (Romans 5:3-4).

The rest of that day I scrawled my prayers across little scraps of paper, writing out every thought in my head and then letting go of my worries with each entry. Some were duplicated. That was okay. Something about that physical act of putting them on paper released their hold on me.

When I bent down to lift my purse from under the desk to leave for the day, an uncontrollable urge to cough forced my hand to my chest. The rumbles produced wet gurgles—a feeling I hadn't experienced before. I tried a few *ahem*s, but there was no phlegm. I hacked again, this time like a smoker. The coughing persisted on and off without any relief.

On a scrap of paper I scribbled, "I'm worried that my coughing is related to my cancer instead of some other sickness."

13

CRACKLY AND WET, the cough persisted until morning. I lifted my hand to my heart and felt the rumble and the familiar weight pressing against my lungs with each breath. Giving in to chemotherapy didn't seem difficult now that I imagined my tumor toying with swallowing my lungs. I had exhausted all possibilities of curing myself.

Two days later, Marge, my boss, drove me across the street to Good Samaritan for my first chemo treatment. I was five months pregnant.

I walked through doors labeled Infusion Center, my heart pounding as if I'd run a mile. Sweat trickled down the sides of my ribcage.

Older patients stared at TV screens. Some hung on to the IV poles administering their second chance at life. *This place smells like death. God help us.* I wrung my hands and pleaded with God to magically heal me. The receptionist interrupted. "Your name, please?"

"Catherine Jones," I whispered.

Saying the name out loud for the first time felt strange. Working at the hospital had its perks, but having everyone know your name while you battled a serious disease wasn't one of them. As an employee, I received special treatment, which, I admit, came in handy when I needed a test right away. But Dr. McGarry said he noticed that my medical records had intermittently been checked out by other doctors—some concerned with my health, others about the choice of treatment plan for such a sensitive case. Dr. McGarry had decided to change my name to Catherine Jones.

A young lady with cropped brown hair walked toward the desk.

"Hi, I'm Lisa." She smiled. "I'll be your nurse."

I told my boss she could go back to work, that I'd be fine. Really. The truth was, I didn't want her to see me cry, didn't want to publicly melt down in front of her. But my heart wouldn't stop racing, and this new nurse looked at me with compassion in her eyes, and all I could think was, *No. Not like this. This isn't supposed to happen this way.*

I looked from Marge to Lisa to the receptionist and felt my chest constrict.

Before Marge left, she hugged me. "I'll be thinking of you," she said.

We walked to an oversized steel-blue recliner where Lisa knelt beside me. "Do you have a belief?"

I wrinkled my forehead, interrupted again from my *God-where-are-you?* prayers. "What?"

"Do you believe in God?"

"Oh . . . yes, I believe in God."

"Do you mind if I pray with you before we begin?"

I nodded in agreement.

She held my free hand. "God, . . ."

My shoulders convulsed first. Then my arms, legs, and feet shook uncontrollably, as if someone were slowly electrocuting me. I cradled my knees the best I could in front of my belly, still shaking intermittently. *Why isn't Jason here yet? I hate his job. Where are you in all of this, God? Save me. It's not supposed to happen this way. I'm pregnant and about to receive toxic drugs. How can you want this for the baby? I believed you'd heal me. Please, Lord. Please . . .*

"Amen."

Lisa pulled on thick, blue gloves to protect her from the chemicals, then wrapped a tourniquet around my upper arm. She pierced the back of my hand with the smallest butterfly needle. My vein rolled.

"I'm sorry," she apologized, and stuck me again.

Another apology. She placed a heating pad on my wrist. Five minutes later, my tiny veins had finally swelled beneath my skin. This time, the needle punctured the vein effortlessly. Lisa secured the plastic IV tube with tape and attached a large metal syringe to the other end of the tube. She slowly pushed my first dose of chemotherapy drugs through the needle, explaining that it would take about ten minutes.

Pooled tears fell. *Please protect my baby. Please, Lord, shield her little body. I did the best I could.* I pressed my eyes closed. *She's yours now.* My stomach hurt as if someone had grabbed and wrung my intestines.

Lisa asked random question after question. I knew what she was doing. I think she knew that I knew what she was doing, but she was smart enough to keep up her attempts to distract me and keep me from becoming an emotional mess.

The nurses' station erupted with laughter. I saw the receptionist put one hand on her chest and the other over her mouth. I don't know what he said, but he gets people every time. My husband, the king of charm, walked over to me with his reassuring smile.

"So, Catherine, what's your sign?"

I smirked, then looked down.

He tried another dumb joke to make me laugh, but it failed miserably. Jason knelt and held my good hand. "I'm here for you now." It was amazing how my medical emergencies drew us closer together and Jason's spiritual side surfaced.

My chin trembled as he prayed, "Lord, we know you are in control. We trust you have the perfect plan. Use this medicine to heal Dabney. Protect our daughter as only you can. Amen."

The tension in my shoulders relaxed. *Why don't I have his faith? Give me that same peace.*

Those ten minutes of infusion seemed like seconds with Jason by my side. Once the IV had been removed and my thirty-minute observation period was up, I stood on jittery legs. Lisa explained that some patients react this way to the antinausea medicine I had received, but overall, the first session was remarkably uneventful.

Lisa waved. "Have a better day, Catherine."

14

I never knew pain could be so cruel.

The chill from the cool leather recliner moved through my body as I pushed on the back to elevate my legs and tried to rest in Colleen's sunroom. I wrapped my arms around my growing belly and gave in to the heaviness of my eyelids for my after-work nap.

Then my cell phone rang.

Most everyone from my small town of Palmetto had heard the whispers that I had started treatment. When your graduating class consists of just 180 students, word spreads quickly.

After experiencing many awkward conversations with

well-meaning people who stumbled over what to say to a sick person, hearing Ashlee's voice brought hope. Only two years earlier, doctors had discovered tumors along her spine, and ultrasound treatment had eradicated her growths, she explained. I needed to hear more success stories to tip the odds in my favor.

"How did you handle being sick? Did it consume your thoughts?" I scratched my wrist until the skin turned splotchy and red. "I'm kinda mad I had to start treatment."

I summarized my plan of failed alternative approaches, assuming Ashlee, of all people, would understand the fear filling my mind—maybe she'd do a little hand-holding and wallow with me like everyone else.

She didn't.

"You know, there's nothing you can do to change your circumstances," she said. "There is only one person in control. It's not you. Once you realize this, life gets a lot easier."

Another chill ran through my body as I listened to these words my mind knew were right but my unyielding heart may not have been prepared to receive. This meant surrendering. Breathing deeper. Releasing control, like a soldier who realizes that no matter how hard he fights, he can't predict every bullet coming his way.

For the first time since my diagnosis, someone was treating me like a disease-free, normal friend. Before Ashlee and I hung up, we talked about work, life, and the dumb toilet-papering pranks we pulled in high school.

Don't get me wrong. I needed wallowers, hand-holders, and lots of sympathy, but God formed Ashlee's words perfectly for my soul that day. I don't think I could have accepted them from anyone other than a cancer survivor.

I curled to the side in the recliner. When I was alone at home, the silence always opened the door to thought-racing.

Ugh, I'm so human. There was me inside me, and God inside me. I had heard this before—that for God to become greater in my life, my selfish nature had to become less (see John 3:30). My daily battle with following a special diet or sipping a toxin-removing tea or projecting my outcome based on someone else's success had entangled my thoughts. I had been focusing on every book except the one that could bring me supernatural peace.

I closed my eyes and slid into position on my knees: *You're in control.*

A groan rose within me. I knew the Bible verse about my days being numbered. No matter how many hoops I tried to jump through, I couldn't add a single hour to my life. *I can't change my illness. Or the baby's health.* My eyes burned from the tears.

Gravitating toward organic produce to rebuild healthy cells was an obvious practical step, but my health-crazed diet could no longer be my god. I knew science backed the benefits of nutrients and minerals. But what science wouldn't stop—no matter how many wheat-grass shots I drank—was that my body would one day fail. The fact is, the first sin in the Garden of Eden had resulted in a curse that will always bring an end of earthly life. *When it's my time, veggies won't be my saving grace. Christ will.*

I flipped through my Bible to a previously underlined passage in Isaiah 43: "When you pass through the waters, I will be with you. . . . When you walk through the fire, you will not be burned" (v. 2). I stopped at verse 5: "Do not be afraid, for I am with you." I lowered my head onto the footpad of the recliner. *It still doesn't seem fair.* I sucked in a breath. *Please give me peace about this. I just want to know I'm going to survive. Isn't that all anyone wants?*

I raised my head, and my eyes skimmed to verse 10: "'You are my witnesses,' declares the LORD, 'and my servant whom I have chosen.'"

Then, three verses down, I stopped cold: "When I act, who can reverse it?"

I bit my thumbnail, knowing what these words meant. God could heal me if he wanted to, but for some reason . . . he hadn't.

I drew in the deepest breath my limited lungs could handle and let it out. *God help me.* I leaned face-forward and allowed my shoulders to shake as I sobbed.

That day was the first step in surrendering my supergirl persona, along with all her imperfections. On my knees, I stopped telling myself I caused my disease with senseless worrying over some crazy, work-related stress. I needed to stop the blaming. No secret to God, because my illness had lined his book long before 1998.

I returned to my journal and reread a recent entry: "Our light and momentary troubles are achieving for us an eternal glory that far outweighs them all. So we fix our eyes not on what is seen, but on what is unseen. For what is seen is temporary, but what is unseen is eternal" (2 Corinthians 4:17-18).

Eternal glory. That's my new focus. *Lord, please help me fix my eyes on you, not on my problems. I assume you have a purpose for my trial. I hate it. Is that all right to admit?* I sighed. *I'm trying to learn how you want to use this cruddy experience. This momentary trouble will pass. I have to believe that.*

I pulled a blanket around my shoulders and fell asleep around seven that night.

15

I surrendered my control issues. Sort of.

By the following Friday, I started a new habit of praying or Bible reading when anxious thoughts entered my head, and as a result, I arrived for my second treatment with a lighter heart and a lopsided smile, the best I could do considering my circumstances. I even let Lisa in on my pseudonym secret.

We chuckled, and she winked each time she said, "Catherine" loudly. "Good to see you, *Catherine*." "What a nice dress, *Catherine*." "What a pretty smile, *Catherine*."

I suppressed my laughter and knew from that moment on that Lisa would become a close friend.

On the ride home, Jason purposely sang off-key while he listened to the radio.

My cheeks hurt a little from smiling so much. I couldn't help but enjoy this happier side of him, this glimpse of hope for our fluctuating relationship. Watching me giggle, Jason reached out and held my hand. Warmth flooded my body.

* * *

Three weeks into my treatment, Jason raced through the front door calling out my name. He found me in the sunroom and knelt beside the off-white recliner, burying his face in my lap. He explained with a quivering chin that he had seen a pair of crosses on the side of the road—one big, one little.

The symbolism angered him so much that he started cutting in and out of traffic and began threatening God out loud, in his car. "I said to God, 'If a year from now I'm placing two crosses in the ground because you took from me my wife and child, I'll never serve you again. I'll do more damage for the Kingdom than good.'" Jason's voice broke. "'Growing up, I did everything you told me to. How can you call yourself a good God? If this is my fate, you're not a God I want to believe in.'"

My heart pounded, and my mouth went dry.

Jason said the car in front of him suddenly stopped short and he slammed on the brakes.

"I needed to calm down, so I put in my Keith Green CD. Guess what song played?"

I shrugged, a little afraid to interrupt him.

"I Pledge My Head to Heaven."

I looked at him blankly, which was his signal that I had no clue what that meant.

Then he sang-spoke a little:

Well, I pledge my wife to heaven for the gospel,
though our love each passing day just seems to grow.

He touched my hand, caressed my fingers as he continued to sing the lyrics about loving his wife but wanting to love the Savior more.

As I told her when we wed, I'd surely rather be found dead,
than to love her more than the one who saved my soul.
I'm your child, and I want to be in your family forever.
I'm your child, and I'm going to follow you,
no matter whatever the cost.

I watched his Adam's apple drop as he swallowed, wiped his face, and told of how he had pulled over on the shoulder and collapsed on the steering wheel, crying. He knew he had heard from God. "I asked God to forgive my bitterness. I would serve him whatever the cost. I was weak. And . . . I asked him to please make me strong for you."

He sucked in a breath. "I don't know how much more . . . I can take." His voice softened, and tears dripped from his cheeks. "But I promised God that I was his child. You were his child. Our daughter . . . his child."

I let out the breath that I didn't realize I was holding and kissed Jason's head, which had fallen into my lap.

When he looked at me a few seconds later, a little more composed, he said, "I *audibly* heard God say that as soon as I accepted the plans he had for your life, then he would heal you. He said, '*Trust me with her life or death, either way.*'

"I told God, 'I'll trust you. Even if I don't like the results. I may not like you for a while, but I'll never stop believing that you're the God of the universe.'" And then the craziest moment in his life happened, he said. "I heard a promise from God: 'Her health will be restored like Job. Your family, land, and livestock will increase. The second half of your lives will be better than the first. But things will get worse before they get better.'"

At this, my mouth opened.

When I realized he was still staring at me, I grinned uncomfortably. I had been a believer since I was ten and grew up in a church where it was a big deal if you raised your hands during praise and worship. This audible-voice conversation stuff was kind of weird. Even though I'd heard from God once, it was a simple sentence, the yellow flower he promised Jason would give me—maybe that's all my simple mind could handle. Honestly, I started to wonder why I hadn't heard the same words from the Lord.

Jason seemed at peace, though. A different kind of look crossed his face and radiated hope. He smiled at me as if everything was going to be okay. Knowing Jason the way I did, I knew he really believed it.

16

When I was six months pregnant, my belly finally popped out to the size of a volleyball. It sat low and perfectly round. I weighed a little over a hundred pounds.

I jumped up from my sleeping bag in the sunroom. My constant shifting in bed and endless scratching made it nearly impossible for Jason to get a full night's rest. I had opted to camp out in the sunroom with my oversized sleeping bag so I could read or watch TV without interrupting anyone else with my restlessness. But this morning, something was different. I stretched and checked the clock to see how late I was going to be for work, since I usually arrived around ten.

Eight? I rubbed my eyes, and unwrapped Jason's tube socks, which I taped around my legs to keep me from scratching at my skin and bleeding in the middle of the night.

I slept through the night? I rolled the thought around in my head.

I felt refreshed.

And alert.

And most assuredly a step closer to normal.

Like an adolescent at her first big dance, I bounced around wildly in the sunroom. *I slept through the night!*

I ran into Jason's room and pounced on the bed. "I slept through the night!"

"What?" He yawned.

"I slept through the night!" I took a deep breath and then realized something else was different. "Wait."

I held out my arms and waited for the spiderlike sensation to creep across my body. "I'm. Not. Itching!"

I jumped higher on the bed, narrowly missing the top of the wrought-iron canopy frame. "Thank you, God! I feel great. I mean, I really feel good. Not tired. Or sore. Or miserable. It's like I'm ten again with crazy energy." I stopped bouncing and chewed the corner of my lip for a few seconds. "I'm taking a hot shower. That's the *real* test."

I hopped down, belly and all, and took my first normal shower in nine months.

The warm water drenched my head and body. Tears filled my eyes. I lifted my hands to heaven. *Thank you, God!*

I arrived on time at my office and used my outdoor voice to tell everyone that the old Dabney was back. Wanting to make up for the days I had slacked off, I ate lunch at my desk and stayed until seven that night. My drive to overachieve was back, along with a smile on my face and a feeling of optimism in my heart.

I had hope.

By the time my weekly Friday treatment rolled around, I was outlandishly vocal. I chatted with Lisa and a few other nurses about the remarkable difference in my energy and how the drugs had worked better than I ever expected. I shared with anyone in earshot that God could heal me by whatever means he chose, and that I would survive the dreaded *C* word.

The following week, a few of the hospital workers whispered that when I started full treatment using all four chemotherapy drugs, I would realize how serious my condition was.

She's delusional. That's what people were whispering.

When I overheard their comments, I inhaled deeply and forced a smile to stay optimistic, to remind my inner people-pleaser that acting happy—even silly—after so many months of misery was acceptable. *God, you're in control. I so want to be a reflection of you.*

As I watched the last of the saline drip from the bag,

I prayed. *God, you say that if we ask anything in your name, it will be granted. I'm asking—no,* believing—*that I won't have to go through full monthly chemotherapy. You can heal me through these weekly treatments.*

17

APRIL 1999

I reread the three-hundred-plus-dollar balance due on the Discover card bill, the lowest it had been since Jason opened the account in college. I scribbled out the number on a fresh check and licked the flap of the envelope. Never before had we paid off a credit card so quickly.

With our credit score higher than ever and our debt finally paid off, Mom and Dad had helped us set aside five thousand dollars for the minimum down payment on a house. The difficult part would be locating something in Palm Beach County under a hundred grand that didn't require major repairs or an armed guard to keep us safe. Our realtor located seven possibilities within our price range.

Now seven months pregnant, I didn't feel like schlepping around town to view houses, so Jason took videos of the properties he saw to narrow the options. The choices dwindled to three.

We drove past nature preserves and county property to Loxahatchee, also known as The Acreage, or the sticks. The area had more dirt roads than paved and more dogs than kids. We pulled up in front of an ash-colored cement building a little bigger than a three-car garage, listed as a foreclosure.

As we walked the perimeter, my outdoors-loving husband pointed out the native pines and the dry, oval-shaped pond hedged with knee-high weeds or water lilies or both. I was too busy swatting mosquitoes to pay much attention. I turned back toward the house to gauge whether this tiny, twelve-hundred-square-foot home was worth such a long drive.

Opening the side door with a push, I stepped into the narrow kitchen/laundry area. From above, a dark, palm-sized object dropped to the floor and scurried under the cabinet. I squealed and ran into the living room and then then let my eyes adjust to the hideousness before me. The walls looked as if a bottle of Pepto-Bismol had exploded and dripped down to the carpet. And if I bent in just the right direction, I could view the entire house from the center of the living room.

Jason walked in behind me. "Nice, isn't it?"

My poker face failed.

"What? Can't you see the vision? Look at all the land, and it's a three-bedroom, two-bath, like you wanted—a perfect starter home."

"Spiders. Mosquitos. *Pink*. We drove thirty minutes from West Palm to be in the middle of nowhere. I'm having a hard time with the vision thing."

"One bug bomb and new doorknobs, and the spiders will disappear. We'll buy carpet and paint. You'll see. Trust me. This place will be beautiful in no time."

We took a gamble and made a bid.

Two weeks later, our realtor called. We'd close on the house in two weeks—the fastest foreclosure he ever sold in his fifteen years of dealing in real estate.

Owning only a four-poster bed, Jason's college dresser, and a toaster after downsizing, we walked the aisles of Walmart looking for lamps and baby supplies. But I was now in week thirty-two of my pregnancy, and my back hurt an hour into shopping. Three Tylenol pills later, we left so I could rest at home.

Jason wrapped a heating pad around my back and tucked me into our bed. He'd sleep in the other room so his snoring wouldn't bother me, he said. But my Braxton Hicks contractions tightened my stomach so hard I wondered how much more my body could take.

I swallowed two more pills and fidgeted, trying to get comfortable.

Around five in the morning, pain streaked across my midsection and back. When I phoned my doctor, she didn't sound happy.

"You're in preterm labor. Get to the hospital."

How was I supposed to know what having a baby felt like? This was my first time, and after all the poking and sticking and sampling done to my body, the cramping didn't feel all that awful.

The doctor prescribed an asthma medication known to relax not only the bronchial tubes but also the uterine muscles. Even though my tummy stopped tightening and my back no longer ached, I was bedridden for two weeks, and all chemotherapy was discontinued. The goal now, my perinatologist, Dr. Reynolds, said, was to get me to thirty-six weeks so my daughter's underdeveloped lungs would have time to strengthen.

Fourteen days of solitary confinement about drove me batty. I couldn't wait to return to work and dig through my in-box.

Until I scratched my leg.

Then an arm.

The back of my neck.

I felt them everywhere, feather-like tickles sweeping my body. Days later, the coughing started.

We had waited as long as we could, Dr. McGarry told us over the phone. Whether I liked it or not, our baby would be born in less than twenty-four hours.

18

MAY 11, 1999

My body was shaking so hard that my teeth chattered. This was the moment, the birth of a baby we had prayed so long for, risked everything for, subjected to unhealthy tests and treatments and experimental herbs. I had no idea what to expect next.

Jason knelt on the tile beside my hospital bed and bowed his head. "God, please . . . ," his faith-filled words flowed. My body trembled.

Dr. Reynolds walked through the door with a smile.

My ways are not your ways, Lord. Help me.

Dr. Reynolds started Pitocin to speed the contractions.

"Epidural . . . I mean, please. Epidural. I'm sorry. The cramping . . . it really hurts."

The anesthesiologist pricked my back, and in a matter of minutes my shaking stopped.

"You're wincing. Can you feel your contractions?" my nurse asked hours later.

I nodded, "A little. Sorry."

The doctor ordered an extra dose of epidural medication, which was wonderful—until the baby decided it was time to come out.

Dr. Reynolds told me to lift my legs on the table.

I couldn't. They lay limp on the bed.

She coached Jason and my sister, who had just arrived, to support my legs.

"Bear down when you feel pressure," Dr. Reynolds said.

"Uh. . . I really can't feel anything," I laughed nervously. "This is normal, right?"

She smiled and nodded. "You're doing fine."

Everything was under control, I was doing beautifully, her voice assured me over and over.

My body tugged forward, and Dr. Reynolds lifted a tiny, whimpering baby. "Congratulations." She wiped and suctioned her, then placed her against my chest.

Madison Faith.

The tears rolled down my cheeks, and I kissed her; my first miracle.

Jason stroked her head, his mouth trembling. "She's beautiful." We examined fingers and toes and ears together. Absolutely perfect.

She shouldn't be here. Thank you, God, for giving us peace so many months ago.

Madison panted quietly.

Suddenly a pair of hands lifted her from me. And like that, she was gone. I looked around as the room filled with people.

"What's wrong? Why are they taking her?"

19

QUESTIONS SHOT ABOVE MY HEAD. I struggled to breathe. People we'd never seen before rushed in with a portable crib and attached wires to Madison's chest and limbs.

"Calm down," Dr. Reynolds said softly.

A nurse slipped a plastic oxygen mask over Madison's lips.

"Everything is going to be okay. Her underdeveloped lungs need a little help, that's all. Lie back; Madison's in good hands. The Neonatal Intensive Care nurses are the best in the field."

Madison never cried. She panted. I wiped my face. Silence filled the room as three-fourths of the occupants left.

I had no choice but to lie there and wait.

Dr. Reynolds pulled off her gloves with a snapping noise. "Where's Dad?"

My sister said she heard someone in the bathroom.

"Jason." Dr. Reynolds pounded on the door. "Are you okay?"

"I . . . can't . . . breathe," he said. "Panic . . . attack."

"Take slow, deep breaths," she said, talking him back to normal.

I was handed a cup with a white pill, the first prescription-strength painkiller I'd ever taken. The lightening effect hit moments later and melted away my pain, my troubled thoughts, and my tension. I closed my eyes, exhausted.

When I woke, Jason walked me to the Neonatal Intensive Care Unit (NICU). We stopped in front of a metal sink, where he unwrapped a prepackaged soap-filled sponge lined on one side with plastic bristles. I followed the instructions on the sign above the sink and scrubbed from elbows to fingernails for three minutes. Then we walked past the tiniest babies, some no bigger than Jason's hand.

Tubes ran from Madison's nose and were taped to her fuzzy face. A mask shielded her eyes from the bright light above. My stomach sank. She was on her tummy, knees tucked under her chest, her left arm taped from hand to elbow with a Popsicle stick to keep her IV secured. Her tiny heels were splotched with dried blood, left over, I assumed, from tests. She lay motionless.

I touched her soft skin. As she squirmed, beeping filled the room, and her monitor flashed numbers and lines.

A nurse made some adjustments, and the beeping stopped. But it took a minute for Madison's chest to no longer rise and fall so fast. The nurse instructed us not to touch Madison until her lungs grew stronger. Each time she reacted to stimulation, her body burned precious calories, and her lungs weren't strong enough to keep up with that kind of excitement.

I stared at her, lying alone in an open plastic box. *I did this to her. If I were healthy, she wouldn't have tubes and wires and bruised heels. What if she doesn't make it? All this time I allowed chemicals to pass through my body to hers. I could have waited longer.*

My brain shut down.

My defense against those thoughts was to separate myself from her. My husband stayed by Madison's side and accompanied one family member at a time to visit her.

For most of the next two days, I slept and visited Madison only a couple of times. That was about all I could handle. I couldn't even hold my own daughter, and staring at her was too painful. That afternoon, Jason wheeled me out to a quiet car.

Once a day for five days, I visited the hospital to drop

off breast milk for Madison. Each time, the nurses encouraged me to stay, to talk to Madison just a little longer.

I was afraid to touch her, afraid I'd make something beep. I memorized her tiny form curled up in the Isolette. *I'm so sorry,* I apologized. I hated this helpless feeling; emotionally and physically detaching was easier.

By day five, Madison was improving, and the nurses moved her to the level 2 NICU. Jason visited with me after work. He snuggled her and kissed on her comfortably. With her breathing tube removed, only a couple of cords remained to monitor her vital signs. I awkwardly held her and even gave breast-feeding a shot. Feeling her against my skin made me smile, and I breathed easier.

In those moments, she was absolutely the most perfect baby in the universe, and as I stared into her blue eyes, I knew that I would fight until my last breath to be able to watch her grow.

20

WE BROUGHT MADISON home after a week in the NICU.
I finally learned how to cradle and dress her five-pound
preemie body without feeling as if I'd break something.
I couldn't kiss and snuggle with her enough.

A week and a half after Madison's birth, she and Jason
kept me company during my oncology appointment.
I had prayed so long for this moment that I fully expected
my doctor to slide my first-trip-to-the-ER films and my
most recent scans into the light box and proclaim—hands
extended—"Dabney, it's a miracle. Your cancer's gone!"

I'd clap joyously and jump about, praising God. I saw
the vision; I just needed to hear the words.

When Dr. McGarry smiled and said something along the lines of, "Dabney, it's a miracle," my heart quickened. "Your cancer is about the same size today as it was the day you walked through the ER doors six months ago." He pointed with the end of his pen, examining the oddity.

My shoulders slumped, and I stared at my misshapen lungs, compensating for the cancerous growth that still entangled them. He compared the films and continued on about the size of my tumor and his amazement at how I had carried Madison so low and how my breathing wasn't affected until the end. He confessed that he hadn't thought I'd be able to carry her past thirty weeks. And he certainly had not expected that I'd be able to wait to start treatment until the middle of my second trimester. He paused. "You don't look as amazed as I do."

"As silly as it sounds, I prayed that God would heal me. I really thought the cancer would be gone." I looked at the floor.

"Did you not hear what I said? Your tiny chest and abdomen carried a 14.5 x 17 cm bulky mass *and* a baby nearly full-term with limited complications. And now your tumor is measuring 9 x 16 cm."

But that wasn't the miracle I had prayed for.

I didn't hear much more of what my favorite doctor had to say, although he kept talking about the new treatment and when I'd start and how the odds seemed to be in my favor.

What had happened? I had believed. I mean, *really* believed this time. Everyone had prayed. I had kept the baby. I trusted God.

Jason massaged my bony shoulders until they hurt, trying to be the compassionate husband. He whispered, "Don't worry. God has everything under control."

When Dr. McGarry left, Jason turned me toward him. "God told me your illness would get worse before it improved. *Then* he'd restore your health." His eyes locked onto mine because he knew from my crossed arms and deflated body that I was playing the pouting game. "Remember that? Don't get discouraged."

My hope—the one I could almost touch if I stood on the tips of my toes and stretched my fingers with the determination of a five-year-old reaching for a forbidden cookie—had been pushed out of reach.

Dr. McGarry had expected my tumor to increase in size each month I waited to begin treatment. I, on the other hand, had presumed my cancer would vanish and God would be credited. But the greater miracle, I knew, lived and breathed and had survived thirty-four weeks until she could be born.

On Sunday morning our pastor brought us forward for the congregation to pray over us. After the service I stood in the walkway with a renewed sense of peace, until a friend pulled me aside. "We've prayed hard for you," he said, patting my shoulder with his weathered hand. "But

I'm trying to figure out why God isn't healing you. Do you think there's any unresolved sin in your life and maybe that's the reason?"

I blinked. "Uh." My mind went blank. "No, none that I can think of."

"We love you guys, and we'll continue to pray. But I feel God wants you to have more faith than this. He can heal you if you truly believe." He smiled, and the creases around his mouth deepened.

I twisted the strap of my purse, trying hard not to let tears fall.

When I arrived home, I thumbed through the Scriptures for some sign that resorting to modern medicine to save my life wasn't a sin.

First I stumbled on John 9:1-7, the story about a man born blind and how the disciples asked Jesus who had sinned, the man or his parents, that he was born this way: "'It was not because of his sins or his parents' sins,' Jesus answered. 'This happened so the power of God could be seen in him'" (John 9:3, NLT). I wanted so badly to encounter that same man at church so I could tell him, confidently, from the Scriptures, that sometimes people go through sickness so that God's work may be shown to others. Only I had no idea what my cancer had to do with bringing God any glory.

Who was I kidding? The disciples, of all people, had

just asked Jesus who sinned. What made my friend at church any different for asking the same question?

But what I found in Isaiah 38 blessed me more than anything else I'd read in a long time. The prophet Isaiah told King Hezekiah that he would die. Hezekiah begged the Lord to save him, and God mercifully granted him fifteen more years to live. Isaiah instructed the king to prepare an ointment from figs and apply it over his boil. The king recovered as promised through the use of a common medicinal practice of the day: a poultice.

That clicked with me. God uses miracles, medicine, or any combination of whatever he likes to bring about his will.

God used different healing methods throughout the Bible. Had he chosen one specific formula for each miracle, my type A personality would have duplicated the procedure. *Spit in mud to form paste. Smear globby mess across the diseased area . . .* In other words, I wanted the easy way out. *God, show me a formula to cure my ailment so I can get on with a normal life, which doesn't necessarily include furthering your Kingdom but will bring about temporary happiness.*

No. God's plans were bigger than my simple mind could conceive.

Relying on him required weakness.

21

Jason nudged me awake. "You're wincing in your sleep. Do you need medicine?"

I rolled onto my back. "Ow!" My hand instinctively reached for my hip where the thick, padded bandage protruded. It took only a second before the blur cleared. *Bone marrow biopsy.* "Yes, please," I mumbled.

The day before, Dr. McGarry had swiveled a needle into the small of my back, screening the marrow to ensure that the treatment plan fit perfectly with my case. And this morning, of all days, I was scheduled to take Madison to her first well-baby checkup.

At the appointment window, I handed the lady my paperwork, insurance card, and driver's license.

The receptionist glanced at me over her hot-pink glasses. "Your daughter isn't showing up on your card. Did you inform your insurance company of her birth?"

"I . . . I can't remember."

"Unfortunately, until she's registered, you'll have to pay for the $125 well-baby visit."

"Oh." I bit the inside of my lip. *Don't get worked up. She's staring. Maybe there's a delay in the transaction and Jason can come up with some money by tomorrow.*

Handing her my debit card, I pretended to fidget with my sleeping baby.

"I'm sorry, ma'am, your card was denied. Do you have another?"

I readjusted Madison's infant carrier on my arm. "Can you mail my statement?"

"I'm sorry. Our policy is payment first."

"I—I don't have money for her appointment today," I said in a low voice. "But I promise I'll register her when I get home. I, uh, need her checked out today . . . because I'm . . . I'm—" I looked down—"sick." My voice cracked at the words. "Forget it. Sorry."

I pushed my back against the glass door to exit and waddled down the corridor, hurrying toward the back of the building to hide. *I can't believe I gave her the card thinking it would work.*

"Wait, hon—don't go!"

I turned to see the woman with the hot-pink glasses chasing me and waving.

Out of breath, I rounded the corner of the building and dissolved into a lump on the ground, setting Madison's carrier beside me. With my back flat against the wall, I felt a shooting pain in my hip from my fresh wound. *Nobody should go through this. God, can't you see my pain? And a lady with fluorescent glasses is chasing me.* I swiped at my eyes and cheeks and was searching for a tissue when she caught up with me.

"There you are. Hey, don't cry. It'll be okay." She squatted down next to me. "What's wrong?"

"I'm . . . a mess."

"It's okay. Wanna tell me?"

I looked at Madison, touched her hand. "I have . . . cancer. My treatments start again in the next week, and I need her checkup completed. I don't know how I'll feel or if I'll be able to drive then."

"Oh, hon—" she put her hand on my shoulder— "listen. I'll talk to one of the doctors. Sometimes they see patients who need a little help. We'll work something out. You wait here." She squeezed my arm. "Promise you won't run off?"

I nodded. "Not a chance. Huffing out of the office with this fifty-pound carrier took all my energy." I attempted to laugh.

"For the record, I think you of all people are allowed to huff out of anywhere you like." She walked back in the office.

I dabbed my face and let out my breath. *I'm sorry, God. I'm so scared. Help me. I just need to know you're still with me.*

I grabbed Madison's tiny hand. She was so perfect. So beautiful. *You're worth going through all of this.* I kissed her head.

Moments later, the back door opened. "Mrs. Hedge-a-guard—did I say that right?"

I nodded, not daring to correct her.

"Come in the back door, dear. The pediatrician agreed to see Madison today. No charge."

I closed my eyes. *Thank you, God.*

22

Fourteen days after delivering Madison, I entered the infusion room for my first full dose of chemotherapy. I was eager to check off appointment dates and put this nightmare behind me. With no babysitting options, Jason toted Madison along with us, only she wasn't so quiet now that we had started her on formula. She screamed— a lot—and most of her formula didn't stay in her upset tummy.

Lisa sanitized the port catheter, which allowed for an instant blood return. Surgically placed beneath my skin and sutured to the vein leading to my heart, the port was raised one-half inch off my chest. The self-sealing material was flexible like a trampoline. She instructed me to take a deep breath as she pushed a colossal-size needle through the center of the port.

One bag at a time hung from the top of a metal pole, allowing the chemical warriors against my disease to drip into my body, seeking to destroy all cells, both good and bad.

Relaxing and watching TV, I smiled as Jason played with our two-week-old. Madison was the most marvelous thing that had ever happened to me. When I stared into her eyes, all my anxieties diminished.

Four hours later, Lisa prepared the final drug, which rapidly attacks cancer cells but equally damages vital organs and is known for stripping years off a healthy heart. Although the drug was usually pushed through a syringe over the course of ten minutes, new research had shown that administering the drug slow-drip style over a forty-eight-hour period would achieve the same results while saving the veins and lessening patients' chances of long-term heart damage.

Over my neck, Lisa wrapped a nylon strap that supported a portable fanny-pack pump. This allowed me the freedom to walk about during the treatment.

Sluggishly rising from the bed, I excused myself to the restroom. I slid my hand along the wall to help keep my balance, but the room continued to move. I reached the bathroom door, braced myself with the handle, and then against the sink.

I clicked the lock and stumbled into the cold porcelain rim. Water beaded on my forehead and chest. My stomach roiled at the chemicals churning around. Then my legs gave out, and I heard something *thunk* onto the floor. I felt pain in my hip, my cheek throbbed, and I rolled sideways on the cold tile. My stomach was at war with the drugs begging to resurface. With a pounding head and my mouth filled with saliva, I tried to reach for the sink, but my body refused to move.

For the first time, I prayed to die.

A pounding on the door intensified the throbbing.

"Are you okay?" someone yelled. "Unlock the door!"

Blessed—or cursed—with an iron stomach that refused to let go of any of the contents gurgling below, I moaned until someone must have found a key.

23

Drugs, something I had avoided most of my life, became my go-to choice for survival. Once dissolved and circulating, they produced a lightening effect that washed over my mind and numbed me into a blissful sensation of floating on calm water. The only downside was the inevitable drowsiness that accompanied it. With two treatments checked off my calendar, I pulled my white down comforter chin-high and snuggled in, laughing as I watched *Friends*, my favorite sitcom.

My eyelids closed until thin, tickling legs crawled across my face. I slapped my hands against my body, kicking my sheets to the side. "Get off!" I ran into the living room.

Jason jumped from the couch. "What's wrong?"

"Spiders!" I wiggled, wiping my hands down my body. "They're crawling on my face and arms."

He turned me around, inspecting me. "I don't see anything."

"One walked across my cheek." I scrunched up my face.

"Now that's a pretty look."

"Seriously." I stared at him, unamused. "Please, help me find them."

Jason pulled back the sheets and searched under, around, and behind our bed. "I don't see anything. I think you're having Vicodin nightmares again."

"It wasn't a *nightmare*. During a nightmare I *see* scary things, not *feel* them."

"You need rest. Go back to bed. You'll feel better in the morning."

Even with my pillow wrapped around my head, I could feel thin legs tiptoeing across my face. "Blech!" I ran through the living room, slapping at everything.

Jason jumped. "What?"

"It's not a dream. They're everywhere. My ears . . . my mouth. I'm not going back to bed until you find them. *Please*," I said with a pleading look.

Jason disassembled our queen-sized poster bed and dragged it into the living room, stripped the sheets, and shook them out.

"Nothing. I don't see anything."

"Did you check the frame?"

Still supporting the box spring, he looked at me as if wondering whether I was serious.

"Okay, I'll check the frame." He walked back into our room, flashlight in hand, climbed inside the frame, and searched.

"I don't see anything. Why don't you take a Xanax to help you sleep? I think those other pills are messing with your head."

"Fine," I mumbled. "I hate this." I walked to the kitchen for water.

"I'll put the bed back together and tuck you in."

"Because that will help, right?"

"I'm *trying* here. What else would you like me to do?"

"Sorry. I feel like you don't believe me. But I do feel something. I'll take Xanax, but you know how I feel about those pills—they put me in a trance."

The next attempt at sleep lasted only a couple of minutes before I jumped from the bed and ran to Jason, dropping into his lap. "I feel them—all over. Please, please, please believe me!"

"It's okay. I'm here." He stroked my head.

I pulled back, searching his face to see if he meant it.

That's when I saw them.

"Your shirt." I wiped my hands across his black crewneck. I raised my hand to my head and grabbed a clump of hair at the base of my scalp.

I gave a tug, and hundreds of fine, blonde hairs released freely in my hand. I shook my head fast, and strands trickled down my shoulders and showered the couch. I grabbed another handful, and it came loose as easily as the first.

Jason picked up my pillow. "Look. No wonder they were crawling in your ears and mouth," he wiped off the strands. "GI Jane?"

I swallowed and nodded. I followed Jason to the bathroom, where he shaved my head as we had planned. The face in the mirror reflected sunken eyes, bloated cheeks, and patches of stubble.

"You still look beautiful to me," he whispered behind me.

"You kind of have to say that, or I'll hit you with the shaver."

24

Sights, sounds, and smells triggered memories, including some I'd like to forget. But every once in a while I heard a song, smelled a particular scent, or passed by my favorite makeup stand, and I was transported back to the still photo etched in my memory.

A visit to the welfare building pushed the rewind button one summer afternoon.

With mounting medical bills, we'd had no other choice than to seek help from the government. Living paycheck to paycheck on a double income, we didn't have enough to sustain us once I took sick leave for treatment. I sat in a chair-filled office waiting to be called when a teenage mother carrying an infant slipped in next to me.

She broke the silence, asking simple questions about my baby, but the whole time she stole glances at my head or the raised skin from the port sticking up off my chest, which I rarely bothered to conceal. She asked the obvious question: if I had cancer. The choice was up to me which direction to take the conversation. Scanning the room, I realized we weren't going anywhere for a while, so I opened up.

She responded compassionately about my situation. Her aunt, she said, had struggled with cancer too. I reassured her that I responded well to the drugs and had high hopes of being in remission soon.

The words flowed swiftly from her mouth: her aunt thought the same thing, she did well with treatment, and was told she was in remission. Then she died.

With her words ripping through my heart, I crossed my legs tighter and tried hard not to cry. "Oh. . . . All I can do is . . . pray my odds are better."

When I looked down at the girl's nubby nails and cutoff shorts and free black Enfamil bag the hospital had probably given her, I realized she couldn't be more than sixteen and was probably just as down on her luck as I was. *Oh, God. I wonder why she's here.*

I never found out. I had had a perfect opportunity to witness, and I had flubbed it up. *Lord, help me to see these "random" conversations from your perspective.*

"Daphne Hedg-ey-guard," a voice called from down the hall. I traipsed into the small office for my case to be evaluated. A black oscillating fan blew methodically across my face while I described my situation.

Everyone had a cancer story, I learned. Because most people had no idea what to say, they blurted out any association that popped into their minds. It wasn't their fault, really. Relating and sympathizing and offering positive words are hard to do when you haven't faced such despair. But when people didn't make up things to say just to say something but were there for me—like Shelley, who dropped off a juicer or visited me every hospital stay, just to keep me company; or the three church ladies who took turns bringing me meals every week for six months; or Nancy, who voluntarily babysat when the effects of the drugs had knocked me flat; or Ronda, who baked her famous chicken potpie and buttery chocolate-chip cookies when she sensed my mood had dipped lower than normal—those honest moments brightened my days the most.

Oddly enough, I felt equally comforted when strangers complimented my ridiculous hat that swiveled from side to side on my head, retold a funny joke while I stood in line at the post office, or gently took my hand at the end of a church service and prayed powerful words over my soul.

Sometimes comfort came in a more tangible form.

One day I got a call from our pastor.

"How are you hanging in there, Dabney?"

"Fine." My voice broke.

"You don't sound fine."

"It's hard, that's all. I'm adjusting."

"That's fair. How are you and Jason doing financially?"

"Uh, we're . . . making it," I lied—to my pastor, of all people.

"Things have gotten tight over there, I'm going to guess. Our benevolence committee wants to help during this difficult time. Next Sunday, if you feel comfortable doing so, bring your bills—car, mortgage, credit cards, insurance, electric—you get the idea. Put them in an envelope with your name on it, and drop them in the tithe box at the back of the auditorium. We'll pay the minimum payments this month and give you and Jason a break."

I didn't know what to say. "I'd feel bad taking the church's money."

"Dabney, the funds are set up to help those in dire need. If we polled members of the church and asked which of them wanted to switch places with you or financially help, how do you think they'd answer?"

"I guess that makes sense. But . . . what if I wanted to buy something like a pair of shorts? Mine are tight from gaining weight with the steroids and all. I'd feel guilty if anyone saw me shopping."

"Buy a pair of shorts, Dabney; buy three if you like. We fully support you. You're going through a difficult time. I can't imagine how you are handling everything, especially since you're not working. We know your heart. You've served in children's ministry and given your time for others. That's why this decision was an easy one."

"Thank you," I whispered. "Really. It's just not easy to accept help sometimes."

"We're here for you. Call us if we can help."

"Thanks."

The church paid our bills off and on for months. Without their help, defaulting on our home and car payments would have been our only option.

Other months, an anonymous cashier's check found its way into my purse, or my sister mailed a large check, claiming she and her husband needed somewhere to send their tithe until they located a church to plug into. Mom visited and purchased groceries and paid for expensive prescriptions. Somehow, extra money showed up and helped us to survive.

I cherished those acts of kindness the most, because that's when I felt the hand of God reaching out to us in human form.

25

AFTER SIX MONTHS of chemotherapy and six weeks of radiation, my body was in remission.

Praise God.

The end of January 2000 marked the beginning of a new year, a new life.

Two months later, pain pierced the left side of my chest just below my heart. It felt as if someone had stabbed me with a butter knife and forgotten to remove it. I waited a month to wake without discomfort and then visited Dr. McGarry, looking for answers.

"Let's run another PET scan. You had an 85 percent

cure rate, so keep that in mind." He scribbled the orders on his pad.

"So, you're not concerned?"

"It could be a number of things. I'll run the test right away."

God, I know I'm healed. I believe you've healed me. Please let this be nothing.

MAY 12, 2000

Four days after my test, the day after Madison's first birthday, I lifted her out of the white crib and reread her wall full of verses my sister had painted. I kissed Madison's sweet face. She giggled and said, "Momma, I owe you," the closest she could come to saying "I love you." So sweet. Such a blessing. My heart could not love anything more than that moment with my child.

At six that night, I answered my phone.

"Hey, Dr. McGarry." I propped the receiver between my ear and shoulder and lowered the heat to avoid burning the burgers.

"Hi." He paused. "I'd hoped to catch Jason at home."

"He's outside with Madison. Want me to get him?"

"No." He sighed. "That's okay."

"I know everything's fine. I'm friends with the tech at the hospital. She said my test looked good."

"She shouldn't have done that—said that. She's a tech,

not a—" the line went quiet. "I've had your results for a couple of days. This is a hard phone call to make."

Through the kitchen window I watched Jason toss Madison into the air in the backyard. She squealed, hands splayed, ready for him to catch her.

"There's no easy way to say this, Dabney. Your cancer's back. It's pretty aggressive. It's spread to the outside of your heart." Another pause. "I'm very sorry."

"What?"

"Your Hodgkin's—it's returned. We can go over everything tomorrow morning, but I wanted you to be prepared that I'm recommending a stem-cell transplant."

My eyes squeezed shut as my knees sank to the floor. My stomach lurched with a familiar pain.

"Dabney? Are you still there?"

"Mm-hmm."

"I'm deeply sorry. . . ." He continued talking for a while, but I never answered.

I'm going to die.

I slid forward, facedown on the cool floor, and heard the burgers spitting grease. Madison's giggles from outside twisted the knot in my intestines. Then the phone, still clutched tightly in my hand, beeped from the disconnected line.

Tears pooled under my face. With my heart and head on the ground, nearly pounding audibly in unison, I turned my forehead from the moist surface, fully flat on the wood floor. I smelled the meat burning and wondered for the first time in months about my diet. Wondered what I had done to cause my disease to return.

Why, God? Why? Why me? I'm only twenty-six! What did I do to deserve this? I want to be normal. I just want to raise my daughter. Is that too much to ask?

I rolled to my side and hurled the phone against the wall. My supporting arm gave out, and I curled into myself.

"I can't do it again. I. Can't. Go. Through. Chemo. Again. Twice was enough, don't you think?" I clutched my stomach. "I hate this!" I screamed. "It's not fair!"

I looked toward heaven, my chest heaving. *Jesus, please, take this from me! I know you can. By your stripes I am healed. Touch my body. Heal me. You've healed others. Why not me? I don't want to die.* I tucked my head between my legs and wept.

I heard the kitchen door slam. "What's wrong?" Jason ran to me, I assumed with Madison on his hip, because I could hear her still giggling, unaware that Daddy was running for a different reason.

"My cancer's back. Surrounding my heart this time."

He dropped beside me. He must have freed Madison, because his arms cradled my body.

My voice cracked. "I can't go through chemo again. I won't."

Madison crawled on top of me and stroked my hair, but my tears and groans and shaking continued even after she touched my eyes and wiped away the wetness with a confused look on her face. Giving up, she wrapped her arms around my body, and in her best toddler words she sang, "Momma, I owe you." She double-kissed my head with a *muah, muah*.

Little did I know that only three months later, *I* would owe *her*.

26

MAY 22, 2000—JOURNAL ENTRY

"I need to start by saying that I love my family very, very much and that no matter what happens to me, I know that I have had the best life possible on this earth. Madison— I love you so much. . . . You make me smile. . . . I pray I can watch you grow up. Jason—I was so blessed when God brought you into my life."

I put the journal down, wiped my face. "You always want to make me happy. . . . You've changed so much just to please me. Thank you for loving me & taking care of me."

A few days later, I slipped into sleep, transferring

power to my surgeon to perform a biopsy of the tumor in my chest. He slit a two-inch incision along my right ribs, large enough to insert the tiny, tubelike camera. A second, staple-length incision allowed the endoscope to illuminate my lungs. Through a third cut, some sort of surgical knife or tongs traveled to pale-yellow, cottage-cheese-looking growths off the sac surrounding my beating heart. This I know, because weeks later, I watched the video over and over, amazed at the sight of it all. A new 2.5-cm nodule grew in the region of my heart, and another, 4 x 2 cm, appeared on the diaphragm, the muscle separating the chest from the abdomen—all signs that my disease was progressing aggressively.

When I awoke, groggy from the anesthesia, in the large hospital room decorated with green palm-tree prints, the drapes scooped back by designer bronze hooks, I heard Jason's voice.

"You're awake." He kissed my forehead. "Happy five-year anniversary!"

My mind searched through the fog to remember why, exactly, I was there. Thick tubes from my ribs draped down the side of my bed.

I sighed.

Surgery's done.

"This isn't exactly the five-star hotel I had planned, but you can't beat the view of the Intracoastal and the Atlantic."

"Ocean view. Nice." I cleared my dry throat. "How'd I get the grand suite?"

"The vent in your last room was open when I arrived. I thought I saw asbestos. Didn't take much to get you moved. Can't take all the credit, though. Your friends at the Foundation upgraded you to the Donor Ward. High tea is at three, and the chef is preparing a New York strip for dinner."

He opened a pocket door to my left and pointed to a green-and-white floral couch surrounded by windows. "I even get my own room with a sleeper sofa."

"Thanks for the flowers," I whispered, and looked away.

"Hey, hey, hey." He stroked my cheek. "Don't cry. We're going to beat this."

He wiped the tears from my eyes. "God gave me a promise that things were going to get worse before they got better. He'll restore you." Jason took my face in both his hands. "I promise. You will beat this. We will. Together. Even if I have to sleep on lumpy, makeshift beds to be near you, I'll do whatever it takes."

"I'm sorry you're stuck with a sick wife."

"God gave me a fighter, not some whiny person who rolls over and gives up. I don't know anyone as strong as you." He picked up the phone and dialed. "Hey, I got you something."

"A cake. I know." I tried to grin. "The nurse told me

on the way to my room. I think she was trying to cheer me—or wake me. Somehow I remember that."

"Figures. How many of my surprises have been ruined?" I laughed.

He kissed me. "Happy anniversary. I'm glad I married you. I mean that."

27

Bright fluorescent lights, goose-bumped skin, a friend offering mindless chitchat—that's what I remember about my first transplant consultation at Moffitt Cancer Center in Tampa, Florida. With my original mass recurring within months of my last treatment and the new spots mushrooming around my heart and abdomen, every day without chemotherapy meant my odds of surviving decreased. With shaky hands I held a sheet of paper outlined with questions.

"Hi, Dabney." My new oncologist introduced himself. "I've been reviewing your files."

He asked questions about my history and performed one of those tapping physicals, feeling for swollen spleen, nodes, or other lumps. He looked at my chart, then at me. "According to your films, you're stage 2A with relapse Hodgkin's lymphoma, but because of the aggressive speed of recurrence and the cancer's spread to the pericardium, I believe you have a 30 to 50 percent chance of cure after treatment."

My face fell. "I'm sorry—30 percent?"

"Well, 30 to 50 percent."

I sipped a breath, praying so hard that my voice would stop shaking. "I was told 65 to 70 percent. What changed?"

He seemed guarded in his demeanor. I could only assume how difficult it was to deliver this type of news. "We create our statistics based on our case studies."

"Oh." My bullet-pointed sheet now dangled from the tips of my fingers. I dropped my gaze.

I could no longer hear him. No longer see him. My thoughts swirled.

I'm going to die.

I slumped in my chair and clutched my purse tighter to my stomach. *Why didn't he lie? Tell me my odds were higher? Give me hope?* I slid my fingers through my hair, dropped my head into my palms. *What would it have mattered if I were dead in a few months anyway? I'll never see Madison graduate. Or marry. Or have kids of her own.* Tearstains appeared on my jeans around my elbows.

God, I need you.

"The good news is your treatment will be quicker this time."

He then explained the different parts of my transplant. The first required a round of chemo per month, but because of the high toxicity of the drugs, overnight hospitalization was required to monitor any reactions and make certain my blood counts remained high enough to allow me to freely walk about in our germ-filled world or withstand an accidental bump without bleeding out from low platelet counts.

Chemotherapy reduces the cancer by loading the body with an army of drugs designed to attack all living cells—red, white, platelets, and, we hoped, the nasty mutated ones. This is something I kind of already knew, but there is considerably more science behind the transplant process.

Once the drugs had minimized my cancer cells, an apheresis machine would extract portions of my blood, rapidly spinning it into separate layers. My immature blood layer—stem cells—would then be siphoned out and tested to identify the layer least likely contaminated with cancer. Using liquid nitrogen, the healthy stem cells would then be frozen for future use.

The second step was the life changer. I would receive high doses of chemotherapy for four straight days. Once my blood counts had dropped threateningly low, to the point where I wavered between life and death, my thawed cells would be reinfused.

Instinctively, the infant cells would travel back to the depleted marrow in the bone, and after two weeks, the stem cells should regraft and grow.

I knew what this meant: infection, organ toxicity, failure of the disease to respond to treatment—any mistake—and the whole process could go south. Or, one missed irregular cell, and the multiplying effect of cancer could again take over.

It's all starting to click now—*I am going to die.*

28

Ten days after my twenty-seventh birthday, I signed a living will that transferred every right possible to my husband.

My stomach tightened at the sight of the brightly lit infusion room with the row of chairs, IV poles, and nurses scurrying around. I winced at the thought of a needle puncturing my new dual ports, freshly inserted above my right breast this time, the site still tender.

After my first round of chemo and planned two-night stay, the nurse informed me midmorning that my counts had dropped threateningly low. My doctor recommended multiple blood transfusions and a third night in the

147

hospital. But my heart was set on leaving, set on seeing Dad, who had flown in from Georgia, and set on kissing my sweet baby girl.

I fought back tears when my nurse pulled out the first crimson bag. *I just want to go home. Lord, take back the breath you gave me, and put me out of my misery.* I pulled the hospital sheet over my head. *I need a transfusion of hope, not hemoglobin.*

Two days later I was discharged with strict orders: no fresh fruits or vegetables until my white blood cell counts increase. Chew sugar-free gum. Rinse after every bathroom visit. Brush teeth with a soft toothbrush and baking soda and salt. Gargle with salt water. Drink lots of water. Rest. No day care for Madison for two weeks after my treatment. Petroleum jelly inside my nose for sores. If my white counts drop below five hundred, go to the ER. And—*no stress.*

I laughed at the last part. My doctor handed me prescriptions for antinausea medication, anti-anxiety medication, an antibiotic, and a drug to treat high levels of uric acid caused by the chemotherapy.

It took only a week before I was swaying back and forth on my bed, groaning.

The thermometer read 102.8. With a fever, a sore throat, and no desire to eat, I headed to the closest ER in West Palm Beach, where a blood test showed my white counts had dropped to two hundred.

Infection.

At the hospital an IV pumped Demerol, a step down from morphine. I was beginning to love those nifty chemicals that rounded off the edges of my discomfort.

Gatorade sloshed in my bottle as they pushed the gurney to a shared room, where a dingy gray curtain separated me and a patient with sickle-cell anemia, who regularly hacked, sneezed, and leaned over her pink hospital bucket. *Poor lady,* I thought. But I hid my face each time I worried about her germs spreading through the room.

The next morning I woke with a throat so dry and painful that it felt as if someone had cut it with a razor. Each attempt to swallow caused me to grimace in pain. My nurse changed my meds to morphine. She handed me a plastic cup with red liquid Tylenol and another bottle of Gatorade.

"I had chemo like a week and a half ago. My white counts have dropped to only one hundred. Should I be in the same room with someone as sick as she is?" I said, nodding to my roommate's side of the curtain. I attempted to swallow the medicine. "Why hasn't my oncologist visited?"

My nurse left to check.

Minutes later, my skin grew clammy, and sweat beaded my upper lip. I grabbed my stomach and groaned.

Rubber shoes squeaked into the room and unlocked my neighbor's bed. "It's okay, ma'am. You can't be in here," an older man whispered.

"Why am I moving? I was here first."

He mumbled something to her, and I heard her say, "Oh, that poor girl," before the room fell silent.

A half hour later my nurse moved me to the fourth floor, oncology ward.

It took another twenty-four hours, until Friday, before my first sips of water and a couple of bites of Jell-O passed my lips. My head still throbbed, and the fever left me achy. By Saturday, after the second transfusion of platelets and who knows what else, my nose, gums, and mouth sores were tolerable. I drank my first bottle of BOOST, enough sustenance to allow me to finally be discharged from the hospital.

Jason brought home Thai soup. I sipped the spicy goodness as I lay in bed and thanked God for drugs, and then wondered if it was okay to thank him for such a thing.

Hours later, I brushed my new growth of blonde hair in the bathroom and watched the strands fall into the sink.

29

"We're inserting a special catheter into your main vein leading to your heart. Did your doctor explain this?"

"Kind of."

"Basically, this catheter allows us to collect the peripheral stem cells that circulate in your blood rather than in your bone marrow. Using this triple-lined catheter, we'll also administer your medication, fluids, and nutrition during your transplant. That way we're not always sticking you with a needle." She winked. "Okay, little miss. You ready?"

I nodded.

"We'll insert the line, then run saline. You'll do fine."

She numbed the area above my heart, then inserted the needle with a guide wire. The cool saline pooled in my chest. She squinted at the screen.

"There's resistance," she called out to her younger assistant and told her to push more saline. "You doing okay, little miss?"

"I'm fine."

"We want to be sure everything's working properly. We're pushing iodine next to see if the X-ray will locate a blockage. Let me know if you're feeling uncomfortable. Just double-checking—no allergies to iodine, right?"

"No, ma'am."

"Don't call me ma'am. You'll make me feel old."

"Sorry." The apology tumbled out. "Habit."

"Now that's the first time I've seen you smile all day. Name's Shirley." Her eyes darted back to the screen. "Dabney, the main subclavian vein that leads to your heart appears blocked. We're pushing a little more iodine."

"Is this normal?"

"Sometimes patients clot at the site where a previous port was placed. We'll find out soon enough. You'll feel another burst of warmth."

Heat spread across my chest. My stomach churned. "I . . . don't feel . . . so good."

"What doesn't feel good?"

"My stomach feels . . . queasy. My head hurts—no—itches." I raked my nails across my smooth scalp.

"Stop the pump! Hives. Benadryl, stat!" Shirley yelled. "Dabney, are you breathing okay?"

"I think. Yes." I turned to my side. "Don't feel good."

"We're pushing Benadryl. You're reacting to the iodine. Throat doing okay?"

"Mm-hmm." Tears gathered in my eyes. "I'm scared." I lay back on the pillow and turned my head side to side, rubbing my skin against the stiff fabric.

"The doctor will be here soon." Shirley caressed my arm.

My body slackened as I sank into the gurney.

I slurred, "Better. I'm . . . feel-ing . . . better."

Shirley patted me. "Good. Little miss, we have to remove that catheter. You have too much scar tissue from your last port. Looks like you developed a clot. Can't even get a blood return. The doctor will explain your options."

"Sure," I said, smiling warmly. "I feel *soooo* much better." I laughed and grabbed Shirley's hand. "Actually, I feel really, really, *really good!*"

"High doses of Benadryl tend to make you loopy. You'll be sleeping like a baby soon. Curtis will wheel you back to your room." Shirley pointed at a large, dark-skinned young man. "Take good care of this one. She's a little woo-hoo—" Shirley twirled her finger beside her ear— "from the meds."

"Yes, ma'am. You know Curtis takes care of his patients."

Shirley shook her head and shooed him away with a crooked smile.

"That's why they call me the big man 'round here. You need help into that chair?"

"Pretty ple-e-e-z." I beamed.

I wrapped my arm around Curtis's thick neck, and he lifted me like a miniature doll. "Your arms are so big," I exclaimed. "Do you play football?"

Curtis smiled.

"See? Loopy," Shirley repeated.

I laughed. "I'm not loopy." I shook my head with each word. "I'm *happy*. It's okay to be *happy*. We *all* should be *happy*. I *like* you, Curtis. We could be good friends."

If serenity flowed through our veins, this would be the feeling.

Curtis sauntered toward the elevator, easing my wheelchair along.

"Curtis, do you know Jesus? I'm a Christian. Do you go to church? If not, you should go—get to know God. He loves you. He even sent his Son to die for you so you could go to heaven." I giggled. "That sounds kind of funny, but it's true."

The doors of the elevator opened with a ding.

"It's so easy to talk to you, Curtis. I'm never this open about my faith. Too afraid everyone will think I'm crazy. I shouldn't be. It's such a great feeling to believe in Christ. Do you believe?"

"Yes, ma'am. We go to church for three hours every Sunday."

"Three hours? Boy, I get antsy after forty-five minutes."

Curtis pushed me along the gray corridor to my room.

"Put your arm around my shoulder." Curtis patted near his neck.

I stared into his chocolate eyes.

"One. Two."

I was in the bed before "Three."

"There. You feelin' okay?" He leaned over me, put his palm on my forehead. "You cold? You're lookin' paler than before."

My eyes closed, and I mumbled, "Never felt better. I love you, Curtis. You are the nicest nurse I've ever—" I grabbed my stomach— "Curtis."

"Yes, ma'am?"

My mouth watered. "I don't feel good. My stomach hurts." My tummy flip-flopped. "Oh no—"

Curtis jumped back.

"Cindy!" Curtis yelled, "Mrs. Hedegard's gonna need her floor cleaned."

He moistened paper towels at the sink. "Here, wipe yourself. You're gonna be okay. Cindy'll take care of you. I'll be back to check on you soon."

JULY 12, 2000

Curtis pushed me to the infusion room as scheduled for my second chemotherapy treatment. A second attempt, with a different type of catheter, would be made once the doctor had reviewed my file.

"I preached at you yesterday, didn't I, Curtis?"

He chuckled. "Yes, ma'am, you did."

"I'm sorry. Hope I didn't offend you. The drugs made me more—uh—relaxed than usual."

"That's okay. We should all be that bold."

"I know." I lowered my head. "Wonder why it's so difficult to talk about something that's changed your life? I guess I don't want anyone to think I'm a wacko or trying to shove something down their throats."

"You said that yesterday, too."

"But I have the most amazing testimony about my daughter. Still, the people pleaser inside thinks my friends will run if I speak that way."

"Maybe you shouldn't be worryin' so much about what other people think."

"You've been talking to my husband, haven't you?" I laughed. "Boldness is not my gift. Maybe that comes with time."

"Or prayer."

"Guess you're right. Guess I should ask God for more boldness."

"You'll do all right, Mrs. Hedegard."

JULY 24, 2000

I returned to Moffitt twelve days later, after my immune system had bounced back from the chemo. This was an important point in the treatment because the success of the transplant hinged on healthy infant stem cells thriving within my white blood count.

Shirley inserted a catheter through the vein in my right groin, only the plastic felt more like a large bullwhip lodged inside my inner thigh. Curtis escorted me back to the collection room, where another nurse draped a ten-pound bag of sand across the tubing to keep me from bleeding internally.

With a throbbing leg, I eased into the hospital bed. The nurse sat next to the apheresis machine. She flipped the switch, and my blood began to circulate and separate into four fractions: plasma, platelets, white cells, and red cells. My nurse kept popping TUMS in my mouth, telling me I needed the magnesium and calcium and to let her know if my lips tingled. This was important, she emphasized.

I woke three hours later with a yawn. "Is it too late to tell you my lips feel prickly?"

She handed me three more TUMS. "You're done for today. We'll see you tomorrow for another collection."

"I'm assuming that means I'll keep the catheter over-night?" I said, covering my mouth as I chewed on a chalky tablet.

She nodded.

With two hands, she heaved the sandbag off my leg. I stood, unable to bend easily. That's when I noticed a ten-inch, eggplant-purple ring around my upper thigh.

I pointed. "What's this?"

"A bruise, I'm afraid."

At the end of the second day of collection, the nurse removed the sand, then the catheter. My leg throbbed under my fresh bandage, but I could still see the large bruise, the purple now mixed with black and gray and red around the tape's edges.

30

The first of three bags of chemo drugs hung above my head while I watched TV.

An air-purifying contraption about the size of refrigerator stood behind a thick Plexiglas wall at the entrance of my room and butted up against my bed. The oversized vacuum prevented airborne germs from attacking my weakened immune system.

I turned the TV louder to compensate for the noise.

My only decoration, other than a few family pictures taped to the Plexiglas, consisted of a large calendar centered on the white wall facing me. August 10, 2000, was circled in red. This announced my first day of chemo and started the countdown toward my rebirthday—the day my transplanted cells added more years to my life.

I knew the transplant time frame all too well. A four- to six-week hospitalization at Moffitt until my newborn cells proved healthy enough to step out from under hospital care—around September 14—followed by a period of isolation in a nearby apartment, with a caretaker, for up to three months, possibly less time, depending on how I tolerated treatment.

Even in the worst-case scenario, I'd be home before December 14. All of this would be behind me.

I clicked the TV off and fell asleep.

"This is Dabney Hedegard, a pleasant, twenty-seven-year-old Caucasian female with a history of . . ."

I rubbed my eyes, wondering who had touched my back, until I noticed my room was full of lab coats.

"She presents with a 2.5 cm mass in the cardiac . . . 4.2 cm mass left . . . 9 x 7 x 16 cm mass in the mediastinum. Admitted for high-dose Cytoxan, BCNU, and VP-16 . . . tolerated treatment. She's undergoing a double-blind study for a new medication," the attending physician read on and on from his chart.

"Blood pressure 90 over 60." An olive-skinned lady removed the cuff from my arm.

After a ten-minute checkup, the attending physician escorted the team out.

A young man with a shaved head entered.

"Hi, Dabney. Name's Chris. I'll be your nurse today." He put the stethoscope to my back. "How ya feeling?"

"Pretty good." I curved my body over my knees and crinkled my face. "Your fingers are cold."

He lifted the scope. "Sorry." He rubbed his hands together, then again placed the circular chestpiece against my back.

"Better?"

I sat taller. "Yeah, thanks. Treatment went well last night. My stomach's only a little queasy. Zofran worked."

He moved the scope to my upper chest. I took deep breaths without being asked.

I looked at the ceiling and tried to think of something to say. "You know, you're the third person this morning to check my lungs and heart. Is this going to be an everyday thing?"

He chuckled. "Afraid so. You're in a research hospital. The attending physician walks his team of research fellows, the pharmacist, the physician's assistant, and nurses in training around to review the cases. Recording and studying your progress by a number of doctors will aid in the improvement of future treatment plans."

He pulled the pressure cuff from the wall mount and slid it above my elbow. "I think constant care like that's a good thing." He smiled. "With all this attention, the chances of their missing anything are rare."

31

With the exception of a swollen right arm, mild nausea, and a twelve-pound weight gain, I had minimal discomfort by the third consecutive day of chemotherapy.

Friends and family scrubbed down and put on oversized white masks while visiting to avoid passing along germs. The few things I remember from that time include Brother Mike praying for me, and my church friend Ragan's mom, a close family friend, feeding me custard pie, the best I'd ever eaten. I never thought real food would pass my lips after having so many drugs fill my body.

When the jittering started hours later, I shifted in the

bed. My heart pounded, my teeth hurt as if they were about to fall out, and my brain felt as if it were misfiring. Ativan would calm the anxious thoughts, my nurse said. But later, somewhere around midnight, my body lurched forward, gasping for air. The lining of my trachea felt swollen, as though there was only a straw-sized hole to breathe through. Grabbing my heart, I drew in a sharp breath. The pain ripping through my chest made my hand smack the bed rail as I fumbled for the call button.

Beep. "Nurses' station."

"I . . . can't . . . breathe."

"Sending someone . . ." The voice trailed off.

I pulled my legs to my stomach, leaned forward, and sucked in minibreaths every other second.

The light switched on. "Mrs. Hedegard, is every—"

"I can't breathe; my . . . chest." I sipped in air with the words, afraid if I didn't, I'd pass out from dizziness. I coughed spasmodically.

My night nurse, Cindy, checked my vitals and placed a pulse oximeter on my pointer finger.

Fading in and out of consciousness, I opened my eyes and saw her push a clear liquid-filled syringe into my line.

As soon as she exited, I punched the numbers on my cell phone.

Jason yawned. "Hey, babe—"

"Call . . . Pastor Dan. Wake him. . . . Tell him pray. . . . Call everyone. . . . Tell . . . them . . . pray. I can . . .

barely breathe. . . . Pain in my heart. I'm . . . scared—" I cried into the phone, my voice escalating on the last three words— "I love . . . you."

I dialed Mom and told her the same; then my body fell limp over my knees.

When Jason heard the line go dead, he dialed the hospital.

"She's frail," the doctor said, "and not doing well. How fast can you get here?"

"Four hours."

"You may not have that much time. And Mr. Hedegard, . . . bring your daughter."

MONDAY, AUGUST 14, 2000

Irregular beeping filled the room when I woke in a fog, a stiff plastic oxygen mask covering my nose and mouth. I felt much like a tattered rag doll clinging to life after a roomful of toddlers had tossed me around and squeezed me so hard that my ribs crumbled.

Peeking through half-opened eyes, I saw Cindy standing at the foot of my bed, staring oddly above my head. The mask pushed deeper into my cheek when I turned my head sideways against my curled legs and took shallow breaths. My eyes drooped closed.

"You had . . . quite a night." I heard Cindy's voice beside me now, but my eyelids were too heavy to lift again. "We're taking you for a CT scan this morning."

She worked quickly, maneuvering me with the help of another pair of hands. Someone hooked underneath my arms and hoisted me into a cold seat. They attached the oxygen tank to the back of my chair as I struggled and failed to hold my head up. Cool air blew past me, and I heard the repetitive squeaks of shoes.

Someone lifted me onto a table, and leaned me back.

I grabbed a hairy arm. "No! I can't . . . lie down. I can't . . . breathe." My body jounced about without control.

"Calm down. We need a CT of your chest. Please. We'll be fast."

They leaned me back again. Tears dampened the hair at my temples; more wheezing, whimpering, and shaking. "Hurry. . . . I feel like I'm . . . drowning."

My eyes shut. I gasped for air. *I can't lie down!* When I lifted my head, someone frantically called into the room, "Please, Dabney. Lie still. Almost done." The voice pleaded, but I saw no one. I just felt precious oxygen leaving my body.

"Two more scans, Dabney." The coaxing voice echoed in the tube.

As my eyes rolled, a vision of Madison appeared. She ran through the yard squealing with Jason.

I want my baby. Jesus, help me. Oh, Lord. I need you. Save me.

The table under me moved swiftly; then an arm slipped under my neck, lifting me. My head pitched forward, and my limbs dangled. Two techs cradled me carefully and placed me in the chair. I felt the breeze against my face again. Squeaks.

So cold. So tired. So heavy.

"Dabney, Brother Mike's here to pray with you," Cindy said when we finally stopped moving.

I opened my eyes enough to see my nurse and the entrance of my room. "I don't . . . feel like . . . visitors. . . . Now's . . . not a good . . . time."

Cindy squeezed my arm. "Now is a *really* good time for someone to pray for you."

A larger hand touched my shoulder. "Dabney." I heard Brother Mike's voice. "I'll be quick."

"Okay," I whispered. My lids fell.

"Oh, Lord, what a precious child you have created. Dabney's an inspiration to others. We pray in the name of Jesus that your presence, power, and peace would heal her and renew her strength. Touch her body. Thank you for her testimony of faith. We're believing you in this situation. In Jesus' name, amen." He gave a quick, soft pat. "I'll continue praying for you. All of First Baptist of Palmetto is praying."

* * *

Jason made it to the hospital and stood at the sink outside my room, scrubbing his arms, hands, and nails for three minutes. Madison clung to his leg.

"Oh, my gosh! She's still alive?" Jason heard a woman's voice behind him.

"Yeah, I know, right?" said another.

"I wouldn't have given fifty cents for her life last night."

Jason cleared his throat and turned, dripping hands raised in front of him.

The first nurse gasped. "I'm *so* sorry—I didn't know you were there. I would never have said that. It's just—I was a respiratory specialist before transferring to oncology. I've seen this situation before." She kept rambling, apologizing. "I've never had a patient survive one pulmonary embolism, let alone two. Not in her condition. Not after so much chemo. I mean—I'm sorry." She paused. "For what it's worth, she's really lucky to be alive."

* * *

I heard a stream of loud beeps; then giggles filled my room.

Madison?

My eyes flitted open. Madison ran through Jason's legs, her soft pudgy face lit with excitement. Behind them stood Mom and my stepdad, Ernie. To their right, my mother- and father-in-law.

Madison sang and skipped around the room. Jason lifted her to his hip while a nurse checked my vitals.

"What's my . . . daughter doing here? I was . . . told I couldn't see her for . . . five weeks. . . . Can't she . . . get me sick?"

The corners of my nurse's mouth raised. "You're doing—" she paused, as if searching for the right word— "good. We thought you'd want to see her after the rough night you had."

My ears rang, and my mind fogged, and it hurt to breathe. But I couldn't help watching Madison stiffen her legs to escape her entrapment. Once she heard my voice, she squirmed down and pattered toward me. I smiled and wiped my cheeks.

My family watched silently.

Madison hopped to my bed, toddler-style, and grabbed onto my sheet to hoist herself up. Jason helped her crawl into my lap. "Momma! I owe you!" Her bare face was just inches from mine.

I swallowed, my mouth dry. "Oh, baby. I love . . . you, too. . . . Momma . . . loves you." I leaned in and kissed her hair, hugged her body close to mine for as long as she would allow—about two minutes. The family members shifted their eyes to something above my head, then back at me. Madison pointed at her picture taped to the Plexiglas and giggled, then scooched back, dangling her legs over the side to drop down.

"E-e-e-e-e!" She ran around the family.

A minute later she climbed back into my bed to play the two-minute hug-and-kiss game. The beeping slowed. Jason looked above my head, then back at me. After a thirty-minute visit, my eyes closed.

*　*　*

I awoke to the sound of sniffles. Fingers pressed deep into my heels. Peeking through one eye, I saw Mom on the edge of the bed, her head bowed and her lips moving silently as she massaged my feet. She worked her way up my leg and to my back, where she started pounding. "Don't you die on me—" Her voice broke.

I don't think I'd ever heard her cry before.

Mom moaned. "We still got many more fights to go through, you hear me?"

"You . . . can't get . . . rid of me . . . that easily."

Mom told me later that after all that back-thumping, I coughed up a handful of mucus-entangled blood. Apparently there was a surveillance camera in my room, because one of the nurses ran in after I passed out and told Mom to stop all that pounding—stop now! It could kill me, didn't she know?

Mom never listened well when she had her mind set on something. No doubt God and Jesus and the Holy Spirit all got an earful from her praying so hard, because she knew only what everyone else was saying: *She'll never make it through the night. Not again.*

Not when they had just injected me with thousands of units of blood thinners to clear the blood clots in my lung. Not with my dropping platelet counts from the chemo. Not when my frail system was unable to fight and they were about to administer my last bag of high-dose chemo. Not with an arrhythmia that caused my heart to race to 140 beats per minute and then drop below 60. Not when my doctors were scrambling to make the difficult decision to thin my blood enough to buy me a few hours to say good-bye.

That night, possibly my last night, my parents had been warned that with so many anticoagulants in my system and so many open sores along my tongue and throat and GI tract, one forceful cough could trigger unmanageable internal hemorrhaging.

32

WEDNESDAY, AUGUST 16, 2000

I wouldn't find out for weeks just how blessed I was to be sipping breaths when I woke the next morning. I watched nurses, doctors, and specialists filter in and out my room, performing tests and scribbling notations on my chart. A big red circle glared from my wall calendar: Infusion Day.

My blood counts were nearly wiped out, producing the perfect environment for my body to receive the thawed stem cells, which we hoped and prayed would be my new lease on life.

But that wasn't the best part. Madison returned, dressed in a mismatched outfit, and ran into my arms for a big kiss. I have fragmented memories of my family lingering in my room. Before I knew it, the sun had started to set.

I had no idea that gastrointestinal bleeding had begun, evident from the first telltale sign of blood in my catheter. Multiple doctors and nurses closely monitored both me and the bedside machine that administered hourly doses of heparin to prevent any further clots from forming.

THURSDAY, AUGUST 17, 2000

After Madison and Jason left from a morning spent resting with me in bed, a group of ladies from Calvary Church placed an oversized gift bag near my lap. Cheryl, the pastor's wife, broke the silence. "The ladies' ministry wanted to bring you something special. They wrapped thirty gifts—one to open each day. No cheating." She smiled. "But you have to get out of the hospital before all the presents are opened, okay?" She tried to joke, but her eyes misted.

I nodded.

"This gives you something to look forward to each morning. The ladies even attached verses."

She handed me a package. "I got you this. It's nothing big."

I pulled out soft pajamas. "Aw, Cheryl, thanks. You didn't have to do this. I can't believe you drove four hours to visit. I'm breathing better now. I even get specially prepared happy meals served daily through my IV."

"Uh, there's a little more 'happy' in that meal than you think." She pointed to the morphine sticker on the side of the bag.

"Ahh. That explains the warm fuzzies, and why I all of a sudden *love* everybody."

FRIDAY, AUGUST 18, 2000

My fragmented days turned into fast-passing nights, thanks to the aid of medication. Much of what went on with my insides I didn't know at the time, especially when two days after my transplant, hepatic veno-occlusive disease (VOD) was noted on my chart.

The high toxicity of the chemo drugs had taxed my liver, and the small blood vessels in that organ showed signs of clotting. VOD is considered one of the most serious complications a transplant patient can face, so my body continued in an unfavorable state and added a new risk: the possibility of liver failure.

SUNDAY, AUGUST 20, 2000

Madison visited me for a half hour each morning for five days straight. Then Jason drove her back to his parents' house, and he spent his evenings watching movies in bed with me. Behind the scenes, his coworkers of only a few months secretly donated their vacation time so his boss wouldn't know of my cancer and the reason Jason often had to leave work with little notice. But now his vacation days had run out, and with no other options, he had to return home to West Palm with Madison.

On Jason's last visit, he crawled into bed behind me and looped his arm around my body while flipping through television channels. I dozed on and off until I heard intermittent howling and heaving and muffled wails in the next room.

"What's wrong with my neighbor?"

"Uh . . ." Jason put down the remote.

"What?"

"Well, his . . . transplant didn't take."

I turned in the bed to face him. "What do you mean?"

"His new stem cells aren't grafting, and there's nothing more the doctors can do. They even used a smaller, backup graft after his first transplant was unsuccessful. I overheard his family in the hall on my way in. He's not going to make it."

"Oh, Lord." I covered my mouth, and my eyes blurred with tears. "That's so unfair. This disease is . . ." *Why him? Why not me? God help him. God help us all.* Jason pressed his lips against the back of my head and held me tight.

AUGUST 21, 2000

Dripping with sweat, I shook as the nurse took my temperature. The lab ran blood work, and an X-ray confirmed the reason for my discomfort: pneumonia.

It was only a matter of time before fluid filled my lungs

and the illness found my immune system in its most compromised state. Concerned with low counts and such a severe sickness, multiple doctors monitored my condition around the clock. With an increase in morphine and more rounds of antibiotics, I slept my days away, unaware how life-threatening my illness was.

It took a week and a half before I was taken off oxygen and the coughing stopped. My physical therapist worked me hard, moving my legs around and rotating my feet. My heart was so homesick and my body so tired of living in a box that I resolved to do whatever it took to get home quickly. But first, I needed to learn how to walk.

Stepping on the hard floor sent thousands of tingling needles through the bottoms of my feet. I attempted to lift my right foot and move it forward, but I fell into my therapist, which she had predicted would happen, because the days and weeks I spent in bed had severely weakened my muscles.

After a few days of hanging on to my IV pole for support, I finagled a way to shuffle around the room on my own. I smelled freedom. Walking, eating, and being able to use the bathroom by myself were all the signs I needed to prove I was well enough to leave my claustrophobic room.

Once I was free of my catheter, I made my first trip to the facilities. Slowly I lowered my stiff body to the toilet but ended up plopping onto the cold seat because that maneuver required thigh muscles, and most of mine had atrophied. After my bout with the pulmonary embolisms, I couldn't eat, and my IV meals weren't enough to put any weight on my bones. Even with my weight dropping, my face and arms were thick, and my skin yellowed and dull. I saw the emergency cord my therapist had pointed out by the commode, but I caught sight of the shower on my left. A new goal popped into my head. Two weeks of rotating nurses giving me sponge baths were getting old. If it meant slow pedaling on my stationary bike and more shuffle-step circles around my room to strengthen my body, I'd do it for the chance to sit in a plastic chair for a real treat like a warm shower.

33

FROZEN IN FEAR, I stood in the dark of night near a row of vacant houses. A musty smell filled the air. *Run!* Something was chasing me.

My heart pounded.

A dark form with a mangled face and an oversized cape for wings swooped down. I heard swooshing. A breeze ruffled my hair, and I ducked. The thing taunted me like a cat tormenting a helpless bug. I lifted heavy legs to run, but they refused to move forward as fast as I begged them.

The cape slapped my face. I tried to take a breath, but the fabric only clung tighter. I beat my head, hands pulling wildly at the parts of the wing suffocating me until I managed to get free and forced my legs to dash toward a ditch, where I lunged face-first. Something smothered my body and pulled my head back. I grabbed at it and screamed. Claws dug deep into my shoulder and yanked me back and forth.

"Wake up, Mrs. Hedegard! You're screaming again." My nurse shook my arm.

I sucked in a breath and wiped the sweat from my head. My chest and back were drenched with perspiration.

I hated the nightmares.

I coiled into a tight ball. My mind was so foggy with drugs that all I could do was pray. I didn't want to sleep, didn't want to be alone, but the hospital was so quiet in the middle of the night.

Turning on the light, I opened my Bible, the only thing I knew would occupy my mind. I prayed that peace would follow with each scribbled note and verse:

I am the LORD, your God, who takes hold of your right hand and says to you, Do not fear; I will help you.

—ISAIAH 41:13

I pray that God, the source of hope, will fill you completely with joy and peace because you trust in him. Then you will overflow with confident hope through the power of the Holy Spirit.

—ROMANS 15:13 (NLT)

God is our refuge and strength, an ever-present
help in trouble.
—PSALM 46:1

Fearful of sleep, I read and read and read.

By morning, half of my notes slanted down the page, some smudged together as if a toddler had doodled makeshift words. The drugs affected my thoughts. My sleep. My memory. But somehow, the wording of the quoted verses, although messy, was perfectly accurate in my red recycled notebook.

The next night, a faceless creature rose high above me, then dipped down until he smothered my face.

"Help!"

My nurse woke me for the third time.

Sweat trickled down my chest. "The nightmares are so vivid. A constant chase. The creatures change shape, catch me, pull at me. I can't take the morphine. Please take me off." I wiped my moist neck.

"You're in a lot of pain; the morphine keeps you from feeling it."

"Please!" I cried.

"Typically we wean patients from the drugs over the course of—"

I shook my head and rolled to my side, pulling my stick-like legs to my chest. "Turn it off."

Hours after the meds no longer dripped, the beasts still

attacked my mind. Pulling and laughing, they cornered me until I screamed myself awake. Sweat drenched my gown, and my sheets were twisted at the end of my bed, leaving me chilled to the bone. Alone and afraid, with a pounding head and sour stomach, I finally shuffle-stepped my IV pole to the bathroom and flipped on the light.

Feeling safe under the bright fluorescent light, I shivered, patting the cold tile wall with my free hand. But my spindly legs buckled, and I dropped to the floor. The pole swung to the wall with a smack. My cheek hit the tile first, and I closed my eyes. My body trembled, and my legs jerked until the chills subsided. A wave of warmth traveled up my spine and throughout my limbs. Sweat appeared on my forehead and upper lip.

"I wanna die. God, let me die," I moaned, tears flowing. *This is worse than all the chemo combined. My stomach. Please, Jesus . . .* My head rocked into the floor.

34

EIGHT DAYS LATER, AUGUST 29, 2000
Twenty days.

That's how long I fought in an isolated room at Moffitt. My predicted four- to six-week hospital stay for my transplant lasted only two and a half weeks.

I learned to walk without the help of my IV pole and slurped cafeteria mashed potatoes and applesauce. My ability to eat a certain number of calories per day was the evidence my doctors looked for to show that I was stable enough to relocate to a nearby sterilized apartment with a personal caretaker. They handed me a big box of white masks and gave me strict orders not to eat fresh fruits or vegetables, because they harbored bacteria. My weakened immune system housed cells similar to those of a new-born baby. They needed time to strengthen before I could resume any normal community interactions.

"Absolutely no dining out for at least three months," my discharge nurse emphasized.

"Why?"

"Restaurants are riddled with germs. After three months, if your counts are higher, then you can eat out. But check the bathroom in every restaurant before you order anything. If it's dirty, then the kitchen's filthy. Don't eat there." She tapped her pen on the discharge paper.

I recoiled at the thought of how many disgusting bathrooms I'd visited. "I'm sorry if this is rude, but how do you know the kitchen will be dirtier?"

"Inspectors. Research. My job is to know what germs may land you back in the hospital. If they're not cleaning the bathroom, which you *can* see, they're certainly not cleaning the kitchen, which you can't. Got it?"

"Ew."

"Ew is right. One last test before we let you go."

The nurse took my blood pressure, which again was low. She measured as I stood, then when I bent over, and finally while I was lying on the table.

"Have you always had low blood pressure?"

"I think so."

She hesitated. "Okay. Everything else looks good. Just

keep an eye on your blood pressure and make sure all hard surfaces in the apartment are cleaned with bleach."

My predicted worst-case-scenario three-month period of isolation in the apartment ended up being just nine days. I credited my stubbornness, a broken heart from missing my sweet baby, and a lot of help from above for such a shortened stay. My total time for my complete transplant was only four and a half weeks.

The chemo, coupled with weeks of bed rest, had weakened my bones and made them porous and fragile. Measuring one inch shorter as a result of osteopenia, the stage before osteoporosis, and weighing in at just eighty-nine pounds, I left the apartment for home on September 6, 2000.

35

I LAY ACROSS OUR new cream-colored couch with tissues crumpled beside me.

Most days following my transplant, I'd walk from the couch to the bed, the bed to the bathroom, the bathroom to the living-room floor, where Madison could run around me. I couldn't play. Walking those few steps used up my energy, so I mostly slept on the floor in her room while she napped.

My breathing slowed, and I coughed intermittently. The chills continued, along with more headaches. I took pain pills and fell back to sleep while a caretaker—I can't even remember which one—babysat.

I hated life. It wasn't fair. I had pills to take away the pain, but they also numbed my thoughts to a haze. Madison ran by with plastic teacups, pop-up books, and her four binkies. All I could do was watch, as if I sat behind a glass wall.

Laundry piled up, smudges collected on the wood floor, and the rings in the toilet grew darker when Jason resumed his hectic work schedule.

After I had been home a couple of weeks, I convinced Jason that I could watch Madison by myself. It took only an hour to realize that she required more work than I had remembered. I lay on the floor most of the morning, questioning God—again.

No. Not questioning—being angry with him. Angry with life and super-angry that I couldn't drive my own daughter to story time like so many other mothers. I imagined my friends laughing and baking and smiling.

I did none of these.

That afternoon, I had used the last of my energy to lift Madison into her white crib for a nap. I walked from her room to my front porch, about fifteen steps, and had to stop to catch my breath. I sat on the cement patio and waited for the panting to subside. *What did I do to deserve this? I just want to play with her; is that too much to ask?*

When the phone rang, I hopped up a little faster than usual, grabbed it from the cradle by the door, and returned to the porch so Madison wouldn't wake.

"Dabney." I heard Ragan's voice on the other end. "We're so glad you're home! We didn't know what we were going to do when we found out you weren't going to make it!"

"What?" I adjusted the phone, not sure I'd heard my good friend correctly.

There was a small pause. "Oh. You don't know?"

"No! What are you talking about?"

"Uh, well—" She gave an awkward chuckle—"Maybe you need to talk to Jason about this."

"Ragan, I'm not letting you off that easy."

"Well, you know, you only tried to die—twice."

"What?"

After much arm-twisting, Ragan finally explained that the night I had sat up in my bed unable to breathe and called Jason, a blood clot had lodged in my lungs and was cutting off oxygen to my heart and brain.

My night nurse, Cindy, had stayed in my room, waiting for me to pass. When I woke in the morning coughing, with heart arrhythmia and my oxygen-saturation levels falling dangerously low even though I was on 100 percent oxygen, everyone scrambled to prolong my life by administering two different blood thinners.

The goal was to prevent another clot, because my morning CT scan had detected one in the lower lobe and a second forming in the upper lobe of the right lung. My doctors knew my blood counts were dropping from the chemo. With my white count threateningly low and my red count falling close behind, my platelets—which I needed for clotting—would dip next. But with no platelets to coagulate the blood and a dose of twenty-five thousand units of heparin a day to thin it, hemorrhaging was predicted to follow. Something as simple as a sneeze could rupture the miniature blood vessels in my nose. The medical team anticipated that with open sores lining my mouth, throat, and GI tract, and vaginal bleeding already started, I'd bleed to death. All they could do was follow protocol, continue with my last day of treatment, and hope for the best.

"They were buying your family time to get to the hospital and, uh—" Ragan's voice wobbled— "you know, say their good-byes." Ragan paused. "That's why Madison was in your room. It didn't matter anymore if she got you sick."

"Oh. *Oh.*" My hands shook, tears spilled, and my stomach twisted.

My red and white counts had dipped as predicted, but my platelets lingered high enough to tolerate a week's worth of blood thinner, which kept other clots from forming.

Supernatural intervention was the only thing my family could credit for my waking on August 16. Hundreds of people across the globe had prayed, as almost everyone we knew called upon the Lord to save my life again. What actually happened around my hospital bed, I'll never know until I reach heaven. But one things was clear: God had intervened.

Then, Ragan said, I fought pneumonia with virtually no immune system left, and the doctors were on around-the-clock watch for my life. "You were a mess, but a miraculous mess." I could hear the smile in her voice. "I can't believe Jason didn't tell you any of this. Everyone's been praying for you."

My knees sank deeper in the dirt driveway. I couldn't remember how I got there, when I had wandered that far from my front porch, or why my hand was tingling, until I eased my grip on the phone.

Ragan was saying something about my daughter. Whenever Madison climbed into my lap, my erratic vital signs from my fluctuating heart messed with my oxygen levels and made breathing difficult. But my heart steadied when Madison's body touched mine as I cradled her in my bed.

When she squirmed down to circle the room, my oxygen levels fluctuated on the screen above my head, and the beeping of the monitors increased. But when she climbed back in my lap for more hugs and kisses, I relaxed and took deeper breaths, and my vitals stabilized somewhat. *That's why people kept staring above my head. They were watching the monitors.*

The doctor had encouraged Jason to bring Madison in every day he could. She was saving my life. I sank farther into the ground.

I saved her life. . . . She saved mine.

By the time I hung up, I was facedown in the yard, fingers splayed along the ground, thanking almighty God that he had allowed me to hold Madison one more time. To smell her Baby Magic–shampooed hair and kiss her face. I thanked him for the peace he had given us in our decision to keep her so many months ago, for my doctors in the tough choices they had made to continue with my chemo and transplant in spite of the fact that all my numbers didn't look good. And for breath—even the shallow kind.

God, I shouldn't be here. I get one more day, more time.

The world looked different.

My head absorbed the sun's rays. When I finally stood, my cutoff shorts fell at the corners of my hips. I walked as fast as I could to Madison's crib and smothered her in kisses. She chortled at Mommy's silliness when I blew raspberries on her belly.

And that was it.

Something had changed inside me. The fact that God cared enough not only to save me from my battles with cancer but also from back-to-back near-death experiences meant his fingerprints were all over this journey, and we had documented medical charts and praying communities to prove it.

Nothing ignited my relationship with God faster than an illness. I'd loved God since I was ten. I was that overzealous Bible lover who regularly invited high school friends to youth group.

Yeah, that girl.

But *this* was different. Head and heart knowledge paled in comparison with this saving-my-life experience that really sparked a Jesus fire. I mean, God could do anything he wanted, and he let me play a part in a miracle. Me—the chronic tripper, dyslexic writer, and nonstop worrier.

Later that night, Jason explained how I had been at high risk of a life-threatening bleeding episode, multiorgan toxicity, and further infections.

"Why didn't anyone tell me these things?" I asked.

"Uh—because you'd stress out over it."

I tried to look angry. "I would not."

Jason arched an eyebrow.

"Okay. Maybe I would." Jason knew all too well that I *would* have stressed over it. And tried to control the situation. And carefully weighed every statistic, obsessing over what I saw as my inevitable doom.

36

MY HODGEPODGE OF drugstore makeup got pitched as my doctor instructed, since lingering bacteria threatened my weakened system. So I headed to the mall with my friend Ragan to treat myself to a bagful of beauty products.

I walked into the store, hat and mask on, sterilized makeup brushes in hand, and asked the young lady with silver eyebrow studs for a makeover.

She stepped back, eyes wide.

"Please," I said, "I just need new makeup. I can't get you sick or anything." I explained about my transplant and how the mask was for *my* protection. Then I caught sight of my reflection in the mirror behind her: pale skin, dark sunken eyes, a large white mask, and a big hat hanging loosely on my bald head.

She mumbled something about not being able to use my brushes.

"Oh." I lowered my head and walked out of the store.

"Hey, lady, wait!" she yelled.

But it was too late. I'd already grabbed my keys and left empty-handed.

People stared, kids pointed, and shoppers sidestepped as I walked by. I promised myself that when I got better, I would make an effort to talk to anyone with a mask, or an unnaturally bald head, or a deformed body. My outward appearance may have looked funny, but my heart still felt the pain when no one wanted to look me in the eye. A simple smile would have sufficed.

Looking different was lonely.

37

MY DOCTOR PREDICTED if I made it a year after the transplant without another recurrence, the odds of my cancer returning decreased dramatically.

We cheered when my first transplant birthday passed on August 16 and the scan was clear. I was feeling healthier and hopeful for the future. But like everything else in my life, once my focus shifted toward a new goal, I ran after it with puppy-like excitement.

APRIL 2002

"I want a baby!" I scrawled across the page in my journal, crying out to God. *Please, Lord—please—I want to be pregnant.*

But I knew the odds. My monthly cycle had never returned after the transplant. My doctor had warned that premature menopause typically followed aggressive treatment, and if I wanted to have any more children, I should consider freezing my eggs. But at the time, I was more concerned with surviving than with birthing more babies.

Now I wanted one more. Madison filled my life with so much joy that I couldn't imagine not having another child, not when my heart reminded me with each passing day that I had more love to give.

Waves of hot flashes, the sensation that someone had unplugged my charger and loaded my purse with dumbbells, and the fact that I craved oversized hamburgers started to play with my mind. I had every symptom of PMS, but the cramping, bloating, and chest tenderness liked to linger for weeks, bringing with them stomach-grabbing nausea. Those were the days Madison got away with anything—or nothing. But when the spotting started, I made an appointment to see an infertility specialist.

Maybe my cycle was returning. Maybe I could have another baby.

"I'll run lab work to check your hormone levels. My guess is that your odd symptoms all point to premature menopause," the doctor said flatly.

"What about a pregnancy test? Will you run that, too?" I asked, gripping Jason's hand.

The doctor chuckled. "Uh, no, I don't think we need

to do that." He looked from me to Jason. "Look, I hate to be the one to tell you this, but your wife's eggs are not viable." He crossed his hands and placed them on his desk. "Even if by some chance she has a cycle now and then, her eggs are chemically damaged. If you want more children, I'd suggest an egg donor. But even then your wife would need hormone replacement therapy, and with her history of pulmonary embolisms, it would be a risk I personally would not take."

I left his office squeezing Jason's fingers and breathing deeply in and out to control my anxiety, hoping that would hold back the tears as we waited for the elevator. *God, I hate my body.*

A week later the test confirmed the doctor's prognosis.

The hot flashes, nausea, and spotting did eventually turn into a cycle every few months as my body produced a chemically ruined egg to remind me of what I could never have again.

Weeks after visiting the doctor and obsessing over my options, I decided that if I couldn't have children, we'd adopt.

That conversation didn't go over well with Jason. He felt one child was enough and had probably been God's plan all along. "I don't think I could love another child the same way I love Madison, especially an adopted one," he admitted. "I'm just being honest."

During much of my adolescence I had lived without

my sister, and many times I dreamed of having someone to confide in. I didn't want Madison to be an only child. So I prayed. But secretly, I researched adoption through the state of Florida and other countries and figured out fees and waiting times and logged my findings on a spreadsheet.

Every time I brought the subject up, I bit the inside of my cheek when Jason repeated no.

38

A MISSIONARY FROM CHINA spoke at our church, sharing stories of caves that house the abandoned developmentally challenged children of China. My heart broke as he told story after story of babies being discarded because of physical or mental flaws. When the infants were found, volunteers smuggled them to caves to be cared for. I left the service unsettled in my spirit. I loved the thought of adopting a baby from China, but as soon as it entered my mind, I pushed my feelings away. *Be happy with the child God has blessed you with.*

One night we ate at R. J. Gator's off Northlake

Boulevard. A little dark-haired girl poked her head around the corner of the booth and waved at Madison.

My daughter waved back.

The little girl popped up, giggling. Her almond-shaped eyes slanted deeper with her toothless smile. The girls played throughout the meal. I pushed my honey-mustard chicken salad around with my fork and stole glances at the little girl's perfect tan skin, dark hair.

Jason finally asked the little girl her name, then began to interrogate her parents with questions about their adoption. "How long did the process take?" turned into "Did you choose your baby?" and "What fees were involved? How has she adjusted?"

I shifted in my seat, uncomfortable. I knew not everyone liked to talk openly about their adoptions, especially to a stranger.

When we walked to our car, Jason strapped Madison in behind the passenger seat and then wrapped his arms around me and sobbed.

I pulled back, searched his face. *What did you do? What do you have to tell me about?* "What's wrong?"

Through tears he told me God had spoken to him. "He told me we are supposed to adopt a little girl from China."

"What?"

I'd put the idea of adoption out of my head for so long, I wasn't prepared for this. And China? My hidden spreadsheets popped into my mind.

"We're going to get this little girl from China. But you need to be prepared for three children. God also told me you are going to get pregnant and have a son."

I winced, then scanned the parking lot to see if anyone else was within earshot. Everything was happening so fast.

Jason drove home the happiest I'd seen him in years.

By the end of the week I had researched every country and narrowed down the list to Lithuania, Ukraine, the Philippines, and China. I created a new color-coded form outlining cost, wait time, and gender of children offered.

I applied to all the Christian adoption organizations, and within a week, brochures and videos were arriving in the mail. I sat with Jason so we could look at them and pray about our decision. He reminded me that God told him to adopt a baby girl from China.

The following Sunday I took Madison to church alone. Jason had played wedding photographer for ten hours the night before and didn't get home until well past midnight. I listened intently to the service. Pastor Dan challenged us, "What is the one step of faith God is telling you to take and you haven't listened?"

As if someone cupped his hand at my ear and whispered, I heard, *Adopt a baby girl from China.*

My lips parted. I turned to see who sat next to me. Vacant seats lined my row in the back of the high school auditorium.

I rushed home with Madison. "I heard directly from

God, like he sat next to me and just said it, calmly, matter-of-factly," I explained to Jason.

He shrugged. "I already told you that."

"I know, but I needed confirmation."

"Took you long enough," he said with a smirk.

DECEMBER 2, 2003

Standing in the kitchen, I poured the usual half water, half apple juice into Madison's sippy cup.

My hands shook.

I grabbed the closest box of sugary cereal and added milk. The food couldn't get into my body fast enough. I pushed the organic flakes with my spoon until I realized I'd only felt this odd, queasy sensation one other time in my life.

I raided my stockpile of tests under the bathroom sink. Fifteen seconds later, I stared in disbelief.

Then I called Jason. "I'm pregnant!"

"I knew it."

Overjoyed, I wrote a poem to surprise our family on Christmas morning. Distant relatives phoned in to read along in unison. Everyone cheered because all those months ago Jason had told friends, coworkers, and relatives how God spoke to him and shared I would have a baby. Now it was coming true.

Our first baby gift arrived in the mail later that week. I held up the one-piece, blue baseball outfit, complete with matching socks. My eyes watered all over again. This was really happening. *Thank you, God.*

By morning, the tinges of blood spotting the toilet paper made my heart drop, but it was the ultrasound that confirmed a missing heartbeat and triggered my emotional crash. My obstetrician ran some tests and then explained that I had a gene-mutation disorder, Factor V Leiden, that increased my chances of forming clots and was most likely the reason for my miscarriage. Because being at high altitudes for long periods of time would increase the risk of pulmonary embolism, I should take a blood thinner or a baby aspirin before long flights and should move around the cabin regularly to keep my blood circulating, my OB-GYN explained.

Things started connecting in my mind—like our upcoming twenty-three-hour flight to China.

39

We'd waited months to adopt. Fourteen months, to be exact. And now the Chinese government had flagged our adoption paperwork. It seemed the term *Hodgkin's disease* was untranslatable and further explanation of my illness was needed.

A second letter was overnighted to our agency, CCAI (Chinese Children Adoption International), and then shipped off to China defining this disease.

China Center for Children's Welfare and Adoption (CCCWA) flagged our file a second time weeks later. We were told that whoever translated my document in China had interpreted it as saying that I had a 5 to 10 percent chance of surviving cancer instead of a 5 to 10 percent chance of a recurrence.

What were the odds of this happening? Hillary, a representative from our agency, tried to calmly explain there was a chance our application to adopt could be denied or postponed for a year and a half until 2005, when I was five years into remission.

We scrambled back and forth between my primary care physician and my oncologist, asking them to write letters on my behalf, confirming the state of my health.

Josh and Lily (Nie) Zhong, the cofounders of our adoption agency, were the first Chinese to own and operate a US adoption agency. Lily practiced law in China, and as soon as she heard about the latest kerfuffle, she retranslated my doctors' letters for us, pleading a third time for the CCCWA to reconsider our case.

Once the papers were off, I knelt bedside and wrote prayers to God: "I feel numb, like someone is playing with my heart—squeezing it so tightly that it burns inside my chest. There's only been one request I've prayed for since my transplant—another child. . . . Please, God. Bring Ansley Joi to us soon. Don't let them take her from me."

The longest two weeks of my life passed as slowly as if I were waiting for a dripping faucet to fill a bathtub.

MARCH 25, 2004—JOURNAL ENTRY
"Yesterday I heard the best news *ever*! Hillary from CCAI called to tell us that they are moving us from

phase 1—screening—to phase 11, the match room!!! We made it! We can adopt! Thank you, God, for answering our prayers!"

JULY 19, 2004

Four months later we traveled to China as a family and celebrated Gotcha Day (the day we "got" Ansley Joi).

Our Chinese coordinator warned all eleven couples that the first days with our new daughters would be rough. She explained in broken English that even though their birth mothers had made a brave choice to leave them in public places—thus risking imprisonment of up to five years—these girls would feel they had been disowned twice: once by their moms and again by the orphanage. "Don't expect a positive response from your children for a few days."

We walked into an open room in the white-tiled government building and saw babies sitting quietly in walkers or held by nannies. Five-year-old Madison tugged on my pink floral skirt. "Mommy, Mommy, that's her. In the corner."

I looked at the child leaning back in a walker. My heart ached when I saw her expressionless face, the shaved patches on the sides of her head, and how flat the back of her head was. They couldn't call my name fast enough. I wanted to push through the crowd, supermom style, and scoop her into my arms.

One by one they announced the names, and baby after

baby cried as they were handed to their new families, turning the formerly silent room to escalating chaos.

"Qian Ping." They called out her orphanage name, which translated as "calm" in Chinese. Dressed in a faded pink outfit and a thick cloth diaper, Ansley was handed to me. Her chocolate-colored eyes stared into my animated face. My voice changed into that all-American mushy baby talk that works so well for other parents, but Ansley's expression morphed into confusion, then fear. Her full lips opened and she released a deep groaning wail—most certainly the loudest noise my ears had ever heard. I did the mommy bounce to quiet my frightened child.

Only bouncing didn't work.

I looked at Jason, who looked at me. Madison jumped up and down shaking a rattle two inches from Ansley's face and singing, "Ansley! Ansley! Look! Look here! I'm your big sister!" *Rattle, rattle, rattle!*

Overly stimulated, Ansley screamed wildly, along with every other baby in the room.

The new parents smiled, coaxed, and rocked crying babies. In the midst of the chaos we swapped cameras and tried our best to capture the memory for our first family photo album.

I pulled out the reinforcements I read about for this perfect occasion. Cheerios? Check. Bottle filled with water? Check. Fresh outfit, light-up toys, noisy toys, singing toys, wipes, clean diapers? Check, check, check.

Nothing worked. Well, the light-up toys did for maybe thirty-seven seconds. While Ansley screamed, we stripped her thick legs and arms out of her clothes and stained diaper, and all three of us helped to redress her in a matching outfit just like her big sister's. Madison loved this idea.

Cleary, the six- to nine-month piece of clothing I purchased would not fit for much longer than the bus ride back to the hotel. The bottom hem of the dress barely covered Ansley's tush. This precious child was not turning out to be the vision I'd prayed for, cried for, journaled about for the last eighteen months.

Nonetheless, we hugged and kissed her mosquito-bitten face and head—half-shaved from where they must have administered IV antibiotics. Commotion and unrealistic expectations and all, the hole in my heart that had wanted just one more was filled with joy.

Ansley Joi.

40

FOUR MONTHS AFTER we had adopted Ansley, friends from church visited to ask questions about the traveling process. They were leaving soon to pick up their baby girl from Thailand and wanted tips. We talked about the importance of bringing snacks, like Cheerios, and toys and such. But every once in a while, Jason changed the subject and shared how God had promised him I'd become pregnant with a son. They nodded and glanced at each other—kind of an awkward moment. What, really, do you say when someone prophetically states that God is going to bring forth a son out of a broken womb?

When Jason repeated this promise for the fifth time, I stepped with adequate pressure on his toe.

Once our friends had left, I started my lecture. "Why did you keep repeating how I would get pregnant with a son? They're obviously adopting for the same reasons we did." I shook my head. "That was uncomfortable. I *get* it. God spoke to you. But you are putting a lot of pressure on me to perform. I can't make my body respond that way."

I continued. "First, you shared it with more than a hundred of our friends and their guests at the men's breakfast. Then with all the people at work, especially the nonbelievers. I just feel . . . awkward when you say it. Please—" I gave him my best pleading look— "stop talking about it."

"I'm sorry." He crossed his arms. "I didn't know you felt that way. I'll stop."

I'd been praying daily for my body to release a viable egg. Just one. That's all I needed. I hid more pregnancy tests under the bathroom sink and liberally tested at the first sign of upset stomach. Emotionally, I couldn't take another negative test. Each time, I prayed so hard for that second line to appear, but after ten minutes of hoping, I'd wrap and tuck another useless stick in the wastebasket. How could one person release that many tears?

Once, my body showed every pregnancy sign: cramps, tenderness, mood swings, nausea for days—I was certain the test would be positive. I stared confidently. After five minutes of waiting for the second line to appear, I knelt on the bathroom floor and sobbed, pleading with God to put my mind at ease.

Am I ever going to get pregnant again? A burning sensation grew along the backs of my eyes, and I leaned into the toilet paper roll. I squeezed my lids shut and bargained with God through moans. *I'll finish the book like everyone keeps asking. If you give me a son, I promise—promise— I won't chicken out this time.* I gulped. *It may sound like a third grader wrote the thing, and Mom and Dad may be my only readers, but I'll do anything. Anything. Please.*

I released my body forward onto the floor. *That's it, God. It's up to you. I can't do this anymore. Either way, I choose to be happy with or without another child. I'm so blessed with the babies I already have, but for some reason this hurts. Wanting something badly and hearing Jason say it's going to happen. I can't even go to baby showers anymore. I'm so selfish.*

I thought I heard words: *Don't worry. Your time will come.* Something along the lines of "You'll have another baby" rang through my mind. I wish I would have written the exact sentence down. What mattered most was that my soul calmed while I was crying out to God.

A week after our friends visited, I called Jason, hyperventilating.

My stomach churned, and my mouth watered, and

I stared at the stick with two lines as I blubbered out the news.

"What's wrong?" Jason entered panic mode. "Is everything okay? Are you at the hospital? Are you sick?"

"I'm preg-naannt! I'm pregnant. You were right. I'm sorry. I should have believed."

I cried for three very good reasons: first, I was in shock. Second, my hormones were fluctuating. And third, Jason was going to gloat.

He told me during dinner that his coworker overheard me flipping out on the phone. "Didn't the doctors say she couldn't conceive?" she asked.

"Yep."

"And she's pregnant again? You called it. I didn't believe you, but you called it."

No one had believed him. But he never cared.

Give me his faith, Lord. Maybe that's why you talk to him. He listens. And believes.

41

Pinching a one-inch section of flesh on my thigh, I pushed the wire-thin needle into my skin, administering my daily shot of blood thinner. I figured the discomfort was a small price to pay to prevent further miscarriages or another clot. But this pregnancy would be different. Normal. I prayed daily that God would allow three things: a full-term pregnancy, another easy birth, and the ability to finally breast-feed.

God could do this.

Monday's ultrasound confirmed a healthy heartbeat. The only other hiccup for the next seven months was my limited lung capacity as a result of scar tissue. I huffed when walking up stairs; I huffed when walking down stairs. Ah, forget about it. I huffed getting out of bed. My lungs hated me.

But I was pregnant.

And happy.

Around the four month, we found out I would have my promised son. This time *my* eyes watered when the tech told us the sex of the baby. Jason stood, arms crossed, a larger-than-life smile across his face. He didn't say a word. He didn't have to.

The next obstacle we faced was agreeing on a name, because my husband's suggestions were all dreadful, like Dawson. And Chase. And other weird names. Okay, they weren't weird; they just weren't the names I picked out. I started baby-name hunting by reading the origins and meanings of biblical male names. "Chase and Dawson aren't even mentioned in the Bible," I reminded Jason one night.

"Who said we wanted a biblical name?"

"I want something semi-normal. I grew up with a name never printed on a single pencil or magnet or mug. And *Dabney* has no meaning."

"I'll create a meaning for you."

"Don't go there. This won't end well." I cocked my head at his attempt at humor. "What about a common name like Jude or James or Luke? Come on. This baby's special. He deserves an extra-special name." I gave him my cute pouty face. "Okay. This one's a little different, but it's my top pick: Asher. It's Hebrew for happy, lucky, and blessed. How perfect is *that*? And—he's from one of the twelve tribes of Jacob." I threw my hands in the air. "Oh, yeah."

I sat back, satisfied with my research.

Jason shook his head. "We're not naming our son Asher. Sounds too close to Ashton Kutcher. Besides, he'd be picked on for the rest of his life."

"I *homeschool*. Who's going to pick on him? The mailman? Whatever. Well, we're not naming our son Dawson Creek either." We both laughed.

That's where the name discussion ended.

* * *

Six months into my pregnancy, Jason wrapped a bandana around my eyes and drove me to a surprise location to celebrate our ten-year anniversary. "No peeking," he kept saying.

I bounced in the seat, so excited. I loved surprises. When he pulled off the faded blue cloth, I read the sign above the strip mall: Singing Bamboo.

"Aw, our first date." I wrapped my arms around him and rose to the tip of my toes to kiss his face all over. He hated public displays of affection, but this time, for this special moment, he didn't pull away. We walked into the mauve-colored Chinese restaurant we had thought was super fancy when we were living on a college-student's budget. Regardless of the atmosphere, their moist General Tso's and honey chicken were the best in town and brought back old memories.

Jason handed me a letter across the table. I unfolded it and began to read.

MAY 27, 2005

I was thinking about how long ten years really is. . . .
I was working at the Breakers. . . . Neither of us had
a degree; the thought of graduation seemed far away,
and we rarely thought about exactly where we would
be ten years from that first date. I knew that all the
chemistry was there. You were young and beautiful,
but shy and quiet. You stared at the sidewalk when
you walked from class to class. You were completely
unaware of how many guys were looking at you
as you passed them. I knew the first time we sat
and talked on the beach . . . that I could tell you
anything. Something inside me knew that I was
in a safe place with you. I could see our history
together before it ever even began. . . .

Details . . . I never imagined that I would
never know loneliness again, unless it was because
you were far away from me while I was in the
middle of the Everglades. I couldn't imagine

owning a house with you on an acre of land when we could barely afford on-campus rent. I couldn't have foreseen my wife lying in a hospital bed without the strength to stand up and walk more than five steps as she fought cancer. I certainly couldn't have dreamed that we would be standing on the Great Wall of China halfway around the world together only four years from the day God rescued you from that hospital bed. . . . I couldn't have imagined that you would still be so radiantly beautiful, even with our third miraculous child in your belly. But here you are . . . still faithfully sitting beside me after ten years. We have learned so much together that I don't think either of us are the same as we were ten years ago.

I know that God's blessing has landed on us as a family, and that even now, we couldn't imagine what the next ten years will bring. I'll write the same kind of letter then, telling you how I can't believe that another ten years have gone by, and that you are just as beautiful as you were ten years ago; and we'll talk about all the things that we have learned and experienced. We'll talk about Madison about to graduate college, and how Ansley is performing in piano recitals, and how Dawson can't wait for us to go camping again with the four-wheelers to our 100-acre farm in Tennessee. Either way, we will continue the journey together, till God calls one of us home.

I love you yesterday, I love you today, I love you tomorrow.

I put down the paper after wiping my eyes. "That's so sweet. Thank you," I said, and hugged him, my head nuzzled against his chest. "You know—" I sniffed—"I never really agreed to the name Dawson."

"What?" Jason pulled back and stared at me. "That's the only word you remembered from my entire love letter?"

"Yep—" I looked at him with a grin, piercing a piece of lightly battered honey chicken— "pretty much. This kid's gonna be born before he has a name."

"He might be." We both laughed.

Then Jason wouldn't stop staring at me, which made me uncomfortable.

"What? Do I have something on my face?" I quickly brushed my lips with the napkin. "Of course, I do." I dabbed frantically from nose to chin.

Jason's lips pressed softly together into a smile. "You're still beautiful, that's all." His eyes glazed with tears. "Happy anniversary."

I gave a little shake of my head. I didn't feel beautiful, not with a big round belly and so many scars from past ports and a shingles outbreak after my transplant.

FRIDAY, JULY 8, 2005

At thirty-four weeks, my pregnant belly tightened regularly. The Braxton Hicks muscle contractions reminded me of Madison's early arrival into the world. With my baby to-do list incomplete, I headed over to the Wellington Green Mall to purchase Onesies and the last bit of hospital pampering supplies, like scented lotions and soft slippers I planned on using for my first normal delivery.

After we had spent an hour in the mall, six-year-old Madison spotted one of those kiddie areas with the over-sized, spongy fruit—kind of like built-in bumper pads—with the perimeter snaked with cushioned benches where mommies could rest. Kids bounced and climbed and pulled the backs of their hands across snotty noses. When each child sneezed, I turned my head sideways and blew out my breath, somehow believing that I could blow the airborne germs away. I had been fighting a cold for a week and a half, and it was often followed by intermittent coughing spells.

By the time Madison had run willy-nilly on every piece of fruit and Ansley hobbled toward the over-grown watermelon—at eighteen months she still walked unsteadily—my stomach was growling.

Suddenly feeling weak, I waddled while Madison pushed Ansley to the food court.

One quick survey of the line was enough to show me

that Chick-fil-A wasn't an option. I turned my attention to the vacant Chinese stand. The smell of fried rice and the free sample of teriyaki chicken tempted me into ordering two plates for the three of us to share.

I shoveled in mouthfuls until my belly ached no longer.

I drove home for naptime and woke three hours later with achy muscles.

Prepped to play nurse and daddy, Jason arrived home from a long day at work. I pulled the covers back over my head and listened to the pots and pans clank in the kitchen. Sometime later Jason hollered, "Dinner's on the table!"

I didn't tell Jason how bad my feverish body hurt. I took Tylenol and dragged myself to my seat, my eyelids drooping. After managing a few bites of ravioli, I pushed back from the table and fell into bed.

SATURDAY, JULY 9, 2005

With a crick in my neck, I opened my eyes in the dark of the morning. Pain shot through my arms, legs, and back as if I'd fallen from a diving board into an empty pool. My ligaments were screaming. I alternated between burning with fever and then shaking with chills. I sat with a moan on sweat-dampened sheets, lugged my legs over the side of the bed, and shuffled to the bathroom. The ear thermometer read 103 degrees.

One normal pregnancy. That's all, please, Lord.

I cried as I dressed for the trip to the ER.

Jason wrestled the kids out of bed and ushered everyone into the van. We made it to St. Mary's Medical Center in record time.

My body trembled while I signed waivers, mumbled answers, and then slumped in the chair at the registration desk. My bones felt as if they could break, my head pounded, and my eyes dropped tears I no longer wiped away. I'd battled pneumonia, bronchitis, and wicked colds, but this felt as if my bones seeped hot poison with each rigid step from the chair to a gurney.

My breaths slowed to shallow sips. But what startled me most were the intermittent gargled coughs that produced pinkish phlegm.

The clack of the brake locks releasing and my gurney jostling startled me. I didn't know I'd fallen asleep. I rolled into the CT room, where the technician stared at my belly. "How far along are you?" he asked, his brow creased.

I groaned. "Thirty-four and half weeks."

"No." He shook his head. He told me he wouldn't perform the test and pushed the bed back into the hall.

My eyes closed. Voices bickered. Someone said something about not being liable for the test. I faded in and out until vibrations and movement woke me and I saw a hand holding a clipboard in front of my face.

"Sign these. For the record, this is not the normal protocol. My orders are for a CT of the chest with contrast."

"I'm in so much pain." I cried and squiggled a line across the papers. "Can I . . . please have something other than Tylenol? My head and body feel like they're going to explode."

"I'll see what I can do." He wrapped the tourniquet around my arm and stuck once, twice, three times to start the IV.

The bed moved out from under the machine once all the whirring stopped.

"Please. Ask my doctor for pain medicine." I could barely swallow past the soreness in my throat. "Please, anything." I clasped my fingers together to tame the quivering and prayed.

He reentered the room minutes later and handed me a pill cup and water. By the time they delivered me to a maternity room, I needed an oxygen mask to breathe.

SUNDAY, JULY 10, 2005
Within twenty-four hours of being admitted, I moved from the maternity ward to a bed in the Intensive Care Unit (ICU).

When the oxygen mask pushed gale-force winds down my throat, something should have clicked that my condition was worse than I believed. I didn't understand the problem. Bilateral pneumonia was the diagnosis, but with four different antibiotics dripping through my IV line, plus morphine, a blood thinner, and medication to delay preterm labor, I would certainly bounce back in no time.

The only problem was that the steady flow of oxygen made my mouth and throat feel as if I'd been sucking on a leaf blower all day. I shifted the plastic mask to the side of my face and sighed, relieved. My lungs felt at ease.

Things beeped. My nurse entered and reprimanded me, then readjusted the mask.

I was craving a Coke. With ice. I kept repeating this to Jason, who sat bedside holding my IV-free hand; that, and I wanted to watch the epidural video. I asked Jason and my nurse and the doctor, basically every warm body that walked in my room, if I could view the clip so I could sign a waiver saying I agreed to the procedure.

Everyone stared at me as if I were crazy.

MONDAY, JULY 11, 2005

I kept forgetting why I was there. No one told me I'd been on morphine since Sunday, which was probably why I felt fine and had only fractured memories of my days.

My husband entered the room. I grabbed a pen and paper and frantically scribbled questions on a lined notepad, most of them nonsensical and my penmanship sloppily erratic. I pointed, tapped at the words Pictionary-style, creased my brow, and grunted.

Jason kept rubbing my arm, trying to calm me.

I pulled the mask to the side to say something, but the beeping started again, and my once-friendly nurse said something about if I didn't keep the mask on, she'd put a tube down my throat and intubate me. Did I understand?

Boy, she's grumpy. Sounds like I've done this before. I nodded once and put the mask back.

I had no idea there were plans to airlift me on the Trauma Hawk to Jackson Memorial in Miami because my situation was so critical. No idea my lungs were filling with fluid and my oxygen saturation level had dipped too low. No idea the baby showed signs of stress.

TUESDAY, JULY 12, 2005

I searched the room for a reminder of where I was. A paper cup with a straw sat beside me on the minitable. A nurse stepped into my room.

Oh, right. ICU. Why do I feel so tired?

I reached for the cup, but my hand didn't move. Straps tethered my arms to the bedrails. My breathing was now effortless. My face and throat no longer hurt from dryness. A plastic tube jutted from my mouth.

Apparently I had tried to pull out the plastic endotracheal tube mechanically ventilating my lungs, so the doctor had ordered wrist restraints. Moving around sloshed the fluid filling my chest, which made everyone scurry to resuscitate me once I passed out from all the shifting. As I struggled with respiratory failure, also known as Adult Respiratory Distress Syndrome (ARDS), the doctors induced a coma to sedate me. My body was too fragile to be transported, and the baby had decided to drop.

* * *

In the waiting area, Dr. Reynolds told Jason they were inducing labor and I would deliver the baby vaginally.

My NICU nurse and family friend, Kathy Edwards, jumped in. "What? Why not a cesarean? Has this ever been done before?"

Dr. Reynolds shot her a look.

When the doctor walked away, Kathy called all the nurses she knew who worked in critical care and asked if a vaginal delivery had ever been performed with an intubated patient in my condition. None had. A cesarean was the normal protocol. But because of all the blood thinners and the stress on my body, the risk of a normal delivery was one my doctor had to take.

My ICU room swelled with ten different obstetric, NICU, and ICU doctors and nurses. Jason's camera panned my limp body, round belly, and roomful of hands working to get the baby out. A new doctor, Dr. Sanford, stood at the end of my bed. "Dabney, when you feel pressure, bear down," she coached me while I slept perfectly still in the bed. "Okay, you're having a contraction now."

With nurses propping up my bent legs, I suddenly sat as if wide awake—only with closed eyes—and I bit down on the plastic cord, following orders.

The doctor saw the head, she said, and maneuvered her hands around the crown, attaching the suction cup to the baby's scalp. Dr. Sanford told me again to push.

My body lifted, I bit down, and the baby slipped out, lifeless.

Like someone unplugged my electric cord, I collapsed back into the pillow.

My son's arms and legs dangled over the sides of Dr. Sanford's hands. She rubbed and suctioned and wiped him the best she could, then passed him from doctor to nurse to the NICU specialist, Kathy Edwards. She lifted my son and pierced his five-pound body with a syringe of Narcan to counteract the morphine in his body. He twitched, opened his mouth, and wheezed while coming out of his drug-induced coma. Someone laid him on my chest for a few seconds and lifted my hand to wrap it around the baby for me. Jason zoomed in with the camcorder. The slits of my eyes opened ever so briefly, but I'd remember nothing about this moment except what the video footage would remind me later.

A plastic oxygen mask was placed over our son's mouth,

and a team of nurses, including Kathy, wheeled him to the NICU to be intubated.

As Kathy stepped through the ICU doors while pushing the portable Isolette, clusters of people held hands, heads bowed, lips whispering away while she walked the baby through what she later described to me as a hall of prayer. Peace surrounded her, and she knew I'd be okay.

Only at that moment, I wasn't.

My symptoms worsened. My body was shifted side to side throughout the day by a special mechanical bed designed to break up the fluid gathering in my chest.

FRIDAY, JULY 15, 2005

My kidneys shut down, and my body began bloating with fluid. The X-ray read that my heart size was normal but the condition of my lungs was unimproved after five days of antibiotics. I was x-rayed or CT scanned or both every morning to see if there were any changes. I remained in a coma. Jason video recorded me every day and waited for me to wake, confident it could happen at any moment because he was fasting from food until my body showed signs of improvement. He believed God would heal me and stated this fact, along with my previous testimony, to the doctors and nurses.

SATURDAY, JULY 16, 2005

Every day Jason asked the doctor, "Are her lungs showing any sign of improvement?"

The doctor always answered no.

On Saturday afternoon Jason walked into my room, weak yet determined, and asked the doctor the same question.

"I don't think you understand the severity of her condition. 'The heart is enlarged . . . worsening lung condition . . . sepsis, septic shock.' That's what her chart states." The doctor shifted on his feet. "Her pneumonia is spreading after six days of the strongest antibiotics we can administer. Studies indicate patients should respond to treatment by day five. Now her heart is enlarged, her kidneys and lungs have shut down, and her body is battling not only multi-organ failure but also blood poisoning. When the organs fail, it's a sign the body is giving up."

Jason's eyes watered.

The doctor went on to say that healthy people die from pneumonia, and that he knew no other way to explain this except "Your wife is not healthy. Her lungs have scar tissue from the tumor, radiation, pulmonary embolisms, and bouts of bronchitis and pneumonia. Now her lungs continue to fill with fluid, and a week's worth of antibiotics have done nothing." He shook his head. "I can appreciate your optimism. However, you need to know she's going to be hospitalized for at least a month." He closed the chart. "But you need to be prepared that she may never leave. Do you understand what I'm saying?"

Jason clenched his fists until his knuckles whitened and

blinked back the wetness in his eyes. When the doctor left, Jason's knees hit the floor. Crying uncontrollably, he pleaded with God to heal my body.

SUNDAY, JULY 17, 2005

The next morning, they increased my oxygen to 100 percent.

Jason's hands shook as he buttoned the back of Ansley's dress. Then things started to go dark in front of his eyes. He reluctantly bit into an apple, fearing he would black out while driving the girls to church. Jason had fasted longer than seven days before, but this time he had made a promise to God not to eat until my body showed signs of improvement. The additional stress in this circumstance put new strains on his physical endurance to complete this vow to God.

Pastor Dan on a whim called Jason from the audience and asked him to give an update on my condition. In front of five hundred people, Jason gripped the lectern. "I don't like the prognosis they gave my wife. . . . I don't accept it." He swallowed. "We serve a God who keeps his promises. When Dabney was first diagnosed with cancer, God shared that her condition would get worse before it got better. It did. Her cancer returned, and we battled through that. But I never imagined there would be another health crisis. God also promised that she'd become pregnant with a son. Today, my promised son lies in the same hospital with the same life-giving tube aiding his breathing that is aiding my wife's breathing. But the third promise God gave me was that the second half of Dabney's life would be better than the first." Jason wiped his eyes. "I believe we serve a God who keeps his promises, and if you as a congregation pray and believe with me, God will heal her and she will be seated with me next Sunday in church."

All around the auditorium heads bowed, and some people grabbed tissues as Jason prayed.

"I want to see Mommy," Madison said after the service.

Jason wrapped his arms around her. "Oh, baby. Children aren't allowed in the ICU. I'm sorry."

"Papa, the last time Mommy was sick, I visited her in the hospital, and she got better. Remember?"

"Yes, baby. How could I forget?"

"Please, Papa. I want to see Mommy. I'll even wear my prettiest dress—she'll like that, the one with green and pink po-ka spots."

Jason's voice broke. "Okay." He knelt, eye level with Madison. "Here's what we're going to do. You go get dressed, and Daddy will take a picture of you. That way when we go to the hospital, if they won't let you in, I'll tape your picture to Mommy's wall so when she wakes, your face is the first one she will see. Agree?"

Madison nodded fast.

She brushed her blonde hair and picked purple, white,

and yellow flowers from the vases filling our house. Jason photographed her sitting on the couch holding her bouquet.

* * *

"Mr. Hedegard, you know children are not allowed in the ICU. The hospital rules are very strict about this."

"Please, let my daughter in for just a couple minutes. We'll be quick, I promise."

"Our patients are in critical condition and could die at any moment. This is no place for a child."

"My wife is one of those patients that could die." He lowered his voice. "All my daughter wants to do is see her mother before it's too late. Please—we'll be in and out."

Somehow he pulled it off. Madison was granted a five-minute visit. She walked through the door and stopped. "Papa, that doesn't look like Mommy."

Jason scooped her up in his arms. "I know, baby. Your mommy has a lot of chemicals in her body making her well, but some of her organs aren't working so good."

From head to toe, my yellowish skin was stretched taut, full of fluid.

"I want to kiss her head, Daddy."

Jason leaned her over me, and her lips touched my skin. My eyelids wavered in response, Jason said. My body was aware of Madison even though the drugs ran heavy through my system.

They taped pictures of Madison, Ansley, and Asher to my wall, then left, exiting through the ICU doors.

"Mr. Hedegard! Mr. Hedegard, wait!" My nurse cornered him in the hall. "I was just about to call you. We got the results from this morning's X-ray, and for first time the fluid in your wife's lungs is starting to subside."

Jason staggered into the nurse, wrapping his arms around her and practically knocking her over. "Thank you."

He pointed both hands in the air toward heaven. "Thank. You. God." Tears streamed down his face. "Thank you, God!" He blew his cheeks out hard. Around the same time Jason was biting into the apple, angry that God hadn't honored his fast, God had already begun restoring my health.

Jason rushed Madison the thirty-minute drive home, dropped her off with my mother, and sped back to the hospital.

Jason signed in and ran through the doors to witness my changed body and nearly normal, flesh-colored skin.

"Mr. Hedegard," my nurse said, lifting two big bags of fluid, "I don't know what just happened, but your wife's kidneys are kicking out fluid like nobody's business. The doctor said he couldn't have given her enough medication to make her kidneys do what they're doing now. And she's not even on Lasix. Never mind. All you need to know is, this is unheard of."

SUNDAY, JULY 17, 2005, 1:45 P.M.

Five hours and forty-five minutes later, my chart indicated that the forced oxygen levels had been decreased from 100 percent to 40 percent.

MONDAY, JULY 18, 2005

"I/O 3130/4000 w/o Lasix!!" That's what my doctor wrote on my chart. In other words, my input of fluid was far less than my output, without medication. Kathy explained later that doctors typically don't write exclamation points in charts; in fact, the only time she'd ever written an exclamation mark in her eighteen years of practice was when she recorded that a woman had jumped over a desk at her.

42

JULY 21, 2005

Gentle breezes filled my room. The flowing gown of the faceless reader wrapped my body in a blanket of serenity. Children sat in a story-time circle—hovering, I thought, because I couldn't see the ground below them.

Sheer white curtains waved bedside, so gentle. Such unexplainable peace filled my heart that my spirit smiled. The reader continued. We loved the stories, the kids and I. We asked for more with giggles that seemed to echo. The reader continued.

In the background, garbled conversations came and went. They sounded like friends planning something.

A woman dressed in scrubs told another she would cover the shift while the other nurse napped in the car. Not to worry—she wouldn't let the patient go unattended. She begged her coworker to rest.

"Another book," a tiny voice trilled.

My soul filled to the top. No pain, effortless breathing. I felt harmony within my broken body. Completely rested, completely secure—abnormally perfect.

I heard hurried footsteps. People moving. The smell of coffee. Someone lifting me. It quieted a little. Then I saw light—or sensed it. My throat felt dry. A bright light again near my face, but not like the shining light from before.

"Dabney, can you hear me?"

Is someone saying my name?

A hand touched my shoulder.

The voice turned away, but I heard bits and pieces. "It may take . . . before . . . opens her eyes, but her vitals indicate . . ."

"Dabney." My chest and back and head lifted some more. "You're going to feel a tug in your throat. This is normal. It may be a little uncomfortable. Ready? On the count of three."

My eyes slowly scanned the room. White curtains. People.

"One, two, three."

One yank. Then another. It felt like a tennis ball being pulled out of my throat. As if scabs were quickly ripped from my skin, a raw, burning sensation spread over my throat.

"Sometimes we surgically remove the tube if it adheres. That was close. Another day, and we would have performed a tracheotomy."

"Praise God."

I recognized that voice. My eyes opened to slits. A face hovered close, his eyes filled with uncertainty. *Jason.* A smile lit his face, his eyes the happiest I'd ever seen.

"You're awake." Tears spilled down his cheeks. "Do you want to meet him?"

Him?

"Dabney—," someone gently touched my shoulder— "do you want to hold your son? Your son."

I heard creaking as the back of the bed lifted me upright. Jason took a baby with brown hair from the nurse and lowered him to me.

My arms were stuck with tubes and wires. I looked down at my belly, the roundness gone.

"My baby," I whispered. "I had my son?"

"Asher." Jason's eyes watered.

I licked my dry lips. "Aw, babe. You didn't have to name him that. You hated that name."

Jason wiped his face and smiled. "You know," he said, "you go through an awful lot to get the name you want."

I tried to swallow the dryness in my throat as I stared at Asher sleeping peacefully.

Jason pulled off the baby cap. "Don't you think it fits him? Look, he has ash-blond hair. I knew the second I saw him he was an Asher. Besides, I hear his name means happy, blessed, and lucky."

I opened my mouth to answer, but the nurse instructed me not to speak anymore. My throat needed to rest.

When did I have him?

That story, I would learn later, echoed through the halls of St. Mary's Medical Center for months. The first time in the history of the hospital that a mom, fully intubated and temporarily coming out of a drug-induced coma, gave birth naturally with two pushes.

* * *

Two weeks after Jason's prediction, I walked into church on Sunday morning. Everyone stood and cheered and wiped their eyes.

"Why is everyone clapping?" I asked Jason through motionless lips.

He waved at the congregation, then pointed to heaven. "I'll explain later."

After church, Jason replayed the seven days' worth of video footage.

"I had no idea. I mean—I never realized how serious . . ." my voice trailed off. "I'm so sorry you had to watch me go through that."

He told me about the coma; acute pneumonia, Acute

Respiratory Distress Syndrome, Acute Renal Failure (where toxic amounts of waste accumulated in my blood when my kidneys shut down), sepsis (blood poisoning, when my immune system responded to the infection by secreting chemicals into my bloodstream), and septic shock (when my entire body shut down from the overload of bacteria). Each condition life threatening.

We'll never know exactly how many prayers were lifted heavenward that Sunday morning when my kidneys suddenly kicked out fluid and my lungs started to clear of the pneumonia. Jason's guess is that hundreds petitioned for God to intervene. My nurse Kathy told me later, after reading through my medical records, "You were dying Sunday and breathing on your own on Monday."

43

ASHER HAD JUST TURNED TWO, and the kids and I were playing in the backyard. Actually, I didn't play. At ten that morning I sauntered near the big cedar swing set, spread a pink sheet on the grass, and lay back in the beautiful December South Florida weather. Asher nuzzled beside me. When I opened my eyes, I looked at my watch.

Eleven o'clock. *I slept an hour?* I counted kids to make sure everyone was safe. *Whew. Lord, why am I tired?*

I tried to remember the last time I'd seen my oncologist. Reaching for my collarbone, I tapped and searched for swollen lymph nodes. Nothing. Fatigue followed me most of my days, but this falling asleep with kids running around was unusual behavior. I couldn't remember being so tired except for when I was sick with Hodgkin's.

I researched fatigue on the Internet. Big mistake.

It could be I needed more thyroid medication, since the radiation had damaged the gland, or low iron, or . . . oh. I couldn't be. When was my last cycle? Five months ago? That was pretty normal, though.

I ran to the bathroom and found a lone hidden test. The second line appeared as fast as the first.

Oh boy.

Given my crazy medical history and my clotting disorder, my obstetrician squeezed me in the following morning.

The nurse slid the slender test strip in my catch container. "Yep, looks like you're pregnant. Congratulations. When was your last date of menstruation?"

I shrugged. "I don't know. They're so irregular these days, usually every three to five months or so, but then I usually have another cycle a week later. It's lovely, really."

"Have you had any symptoms?" she asked while prepping the Doppler with gel and then rolling the wand over my belly.

"I'm nauseous, but I often feel that way before—"

Thump-*thump*, thump-*thump*.

"Sounds like you're nearing your third month."

"What?"

She was right. The ultrasound confirmed that I was eleven weeks pregnant.

Good night, how had I not known this?

Lord, I prayed on a daily basis, *please let the pregnancy be normal. I just want to carry one baby full term and actually nurse one.* With Madison, I didn't have a choice because of the chemo treatments. With Asher, my body was still recovering, and my milk dried up because of the medication. I could never pump more than two ounces at a time for him.

Every other week I schlepped my three kids to my doctor appointments. At twenty-eight weeks, my visits increased to every week, then twice a week. My kids knew the routine. They ate Chick-fil-A while Mom sat hooked to a stress monitor to ensure that the baby's health continued strong.

At thirty-five weeks, I failed the stress test, and my nurse walked me to the next room for an ultrasound, which indicated my amniotic fluid was low. My doctor instructed me to increase my water intake and visit her again first thing in the morning. If the fluid was still low, she would schedule a cesarean, because the baby was flipped butt down: breech.

I did everything my doctor suggested, including rocking on my hands and knees to see if the baby's position shifted. All the while, I prayed. I mean, I really prayed her tiny body would rotate with all that ridiculous back-and-forth motion I attempted while I sucked down bottles of water. I was not having this baby early, not if I could help it. And I certainly wasn't having a C-section.

"You're having this baby today, and I'm afraid she hasn't flipped," my doctor said the next morning after another ultrasound.

Jason drove me to Wellington Regional, and I was quickly suited up in my room. The shaking started first, then the tears, then the contractions. Apparently my doctor was right. This baby was coming whether I was ready or not.

I waddled behind my favorite OB as she led us to the operating room. That was really weird. Where was my gurney? Or my wheelchair? I climbed into bed with Jason's help and leaned forward for the anesthesiologist to insert the numbing medication. They lowered me slowly onto the table, where I lay beneath a large disc lamp emanating glorious heat over my body.

Dr. Walker configured the blue sheet to shield us from the action. "I'll start as soon as the other doctor arrives." I'm certain I saw her smile behind her mask.

"Mrs. Hedegard, you should feel pretty good any minute now," the anesthesiologist said.

The room warmed and my body relaxed. I suddenly felt transported to a tropical island.

Jason lips brushed my head.

Dr. Walker said hello to someone. I turned to tell Jason this wasn't so bad after all, being super numb, not having do any work. Then I felt tugs, and Dr. Walker lifted my daughter above the curtain.

"She's out?" I said, confused. Lovely first words for my fourth child. I heard soft cries. She made noise! My other babies never cried at birth.

Dr. Walker wiped Sabal Grace and handed her to me. I felt more pulling while she rearranged my organs. Dr. Walker told the other doctor, "Go to lunch. I'm taking extra time stitching her up."

Easiest birth. Healthiest baby. *Thank you, Jesus.* I prayed over sweet Sabal Grace, the only name Jason and I agreed on in one afternoon. Named after Cape Sable in the Everglades, a place Jason often referred to as heaven on earth. After a weekend kayak excursion he made me promise if we ever had another girl we'd name her after God's country—you know, with alligators and moss and miles of water. I had laughed at that, knowing my odds of another pregnancy were slim. "Sure, babe. I promise." But spelling the name like the car or the animal wasn't going to happen. We settled on replicating the spelling of Florida's state tree, the sabal palm.

Although Sabal made the most noise, she, too, needed extra oxygen and the assistance of the NICU and intubation and the jaundice light. But by this time, I was a pro at hanging out in hospitals, so the NICU wasn't as scary. I spent four relaxing days in the delivery-and-recovery ward walking back and forth to visit and talk to my sweet baby girl. At last I could thank God for one seminormal pregnancy without crazy health crises, and I had plenty of time to chat up the representative from La Leche League and ask her why my milk still hadn't come in. She pulled an oversized medical book from the shelf.

"You had chest radiation, didn't you?"

"Yes."

She flipped through the pages. "Ah, here it is. Sixty to 80 percent of breast-cancer patients who endured radiation experience blocked mammary ducts." She slid her reading glasses from her face. "I'm gonna bet most of your ducts have scar tissue from the radiation; that's why you're unable to pump more than two ounces at a time."

I bit my lower lip and gave a quick nod. "Thank you."

I had a long talk with God. The idea of using formula really upset me. Especially given my history with cancer and the fact that I wanted to do the best I could to get my babies off to a healthy start. I thought wanting to breast-feed this baby was kind of a simple request.

Jason and the kids checked me out of the hospital later that day without Sabal. Determined to give it my all, I found the nearest pharmacy and rented a hospital-grade breast pump. There was still a chance my milk could come in, I kept telling myself, but I'd never find out, because around six the next morning, the panting started.

I sat straight up. *Can't breathe.* Grabbed my chest. *Can't breathe.* Elbowed Jason. *Can't breathe.* That familiar drowning discomfort had returned. *No.* I attempted to lie back again. *Please, God, no. Not another clot.*

With each vertebra I lowered onto my pillow, my lungs struggled to supply enough oxygen. *God, help me.*

"Hospital," I gasped. "ER. Pulmonary . . . embolism."

Jason rushed the family to Wellington Regional and dropped me outside of the ER while he parked. I caught a glimpse of a mother wheeled out with a bundled baby, pink balloons, and flowers, and a doting father assisting her into the car. I shook my head.

I tapped all my information into the ER database's touch-screen monitor: dizziness, chest pain, shortness of breath, previous history of cancer x 2, pulmonary embolism, acute pneumonia, ARDS, kidney failure . . .

Before I could finish, a nurse whipped around the corner and escorted me to the closest gurney, where a young tech asked endless questions about my health, past infections, radiation scar tissue, and on and on.

They had started with an EKG just as another tech entered with a pushcart and a machine with a large monitor. The techs swapped positions, and he adjusted me on my side and slid his gelled wand around on my chest, clicking pictures and rapidly asking questions. "Any history of heart disease in your family?"

"Yes. Both my parents . . . have had open-heart surgery." While I explained, a nurse wrapped a new ID band above Sabal's birth-mother band. A third nurse started an IV. Puncture marks from the day before dotted the back of my hand.

Conversations flowed between them, over me. They all looked too young to be playing around with my illnesses. I blinked back tears.

A number of doctors visited, asked questions. They read through the list of my physicians: oncologist/hematologist, endocrinologist, perinatologist, obstetrician/gynecologist, pulmonologist. That was all I could remember at the time.

"Who's your primary care physician?"

"Do I need . . . one of . . . those, too?" My attempt at humor didn't go over well. "I visit my . . . oncologist, Dr. Schwartz . . . when I need . . . something." My head spun suddenly. "I . . . don't feel . . . good."

Goo and plastic hit my leg—I assumed for an ultrasound in search of another deep-vein thrombosis, which had caused my last PE. A nurse took blood samples, in search of another infectious disease, I overheard her say. The back of the table lifted, and they told me to sit still. The X-ray jolted my eyes open. I'm sure they had warned me, but I knew the routine. They were searching for pneumonia, PE, bronchitis. And then that word I always hated: *Hodgkin's*. Tapping, pushing, sticking, oxygen mask— I rested in numbness.

After premedicating for my allergy to iodine, they pushed my gurney down the brightly lit hall. Another moving bed carrying a woman I guessed to be in her late seventies was wheeled in front of me. The woman's eyes were sunken, her skin as pale as mine. An oxygen tank, wires attached every which way. A scared look on her face. The room she exited was my next destination. CT scan.

Wow. I swallowed the lump in my throat. *Will I make it to her age? Not at the rate I'm visiting emergency rooms, I won't.*

I closed my eyes as they scanned, trying my best to lie still, my erratic breathing and sniffling drowned out by the loud whooshing noises.

I'm done. Surrendered. My body's failed so many times. Another tear escaped. *I get it, God. This isn't about me. Has nothing to do with me but with what you want to do through me. At this point, I'll do whatever you want. Use me or take me.* I let out my breath as instructed by the tech.

What if I don't go home? What if this is really it? What legacy am I leaving? Will my kids know what miracles they are? My eyes opened. *Not if I'm dead, they won't.*

I attempted a second gulp of air like they asked, then gasped and gripped the sides of the table. Dizziness washed over me.

God, whatever this is, you're bigger. I really get it this time. I promise—I'll finish the book, just let me see my babies one last time.

44

I spent five days in the ICU, undergoing multiple tests and medical reviews. By the time a slew of physicians had finished examining me, I had been diagnosed with congestive heart failure.

I wasn't sure what that meant except that the chemo side effects my doctors had often warned me about had found my heart nine years later, just about the time the doctors had predicted.

JUNE 2008

A sluggish mess. That's what I was.

No amount of caffeine could jolt my weakened body

out of exhaustion. I knew this because I tried drinking cup after cup. Snuffed out, bone weary, oppressed. And compiling a complete thought? Forget about it. Jason listened patiently each time I paused midsentence to remember my original purpose for speaking. Most of the time, I forgot what I'd meant to say.

This wasn't living; it was just *being*: occupying space the way a throw pillow occupies a couch, except the pillow usually beautifies a home. At least the pillow had a purpose.

I plopped from chair to couch to bed and slept the best ever in years. Stiff lungs. That's what it felt like. Each inhale required work, and when I had to use a spirometer to measure my lung function, the little silver ball never made it even halfway up the plastic tube as it was supposed to. Blow harder, my pulmonary specialist would chant. I'd glare at him, wanting to say words I knew I'd never speak aloud. It hurt to blow hard. Didn't they know that?

JULY 2008

One month after leaving the hospital, I slouched in the cardiologist's waiting area, barely able to keep my head upright. I breathed in and out as best I could without inducing another dizzy spell. Wires hooked around my chest and connected to a Holter monitor that continuously recorded a twenty-four-hour EKG reading for my doctor's review.

The nurse called me back, unhooked the portable machine, and then observed my stress response while I jogged on the treadmill with wired patches taped on my skin.

A half hour later, I sat in front of my ICU cardiologist while he confirmed my heart diseases: mitral valve prolapse (MVP) and cardiomyopathy. MVP, he explained while entering information on his laptop, affects 5 to 15 percent of the population, making it one of the most common heart-valve complications in the world.

This didn't sound so bad.

Then, with his thick accent, he explained that there were three different stages of the disease. I had severe MVP. Three of my four valves not only leaked but also regurgitated blood backward into my heart.

"Normal functioning valves allow blood flow from the left atrium to the left ventricle by closing tightly with the pumping of the heart," he said.

My valves expanded with each beat, but then they buckled back (prolapsed) and never closed tightly enough to prevent blood from escaping. This decreased blood flow meant that not enough of the vital fluid circulated throughout my system to allow me to function properly. To compensate, my heart pumped harder. With seeping valves, the fluid pressure began building in my lungs and weakened my heart further. This exacerbation, he believed, induced the congestive heart failure.

That sounded bad.

Still foggy from low blood circulation, I listened intently as he said not to worry. They could operate and replace my buckling valves with mechanical ones. On the other hand, my enlarged heart from the cardiomyopathy concerned him. Many things could have caused this disease: chemotherapy, radiation to the chest, pregnancy, weakened valves, thyroid disease, viral infections.

"Cardiomyopathy," he said, peering through his metal-rimmed glasses, "is predicted to worsen over time." He pushed back, looked at me. "A heart transplant is a viable option later for conditions such as this."

My face fell. I shook my head a little, but I doubt he noticed. He resumed pressing keys on the laptop.

"Your valves we can strengthen with medication." He paused. "But the enlargement—there's nothing we can do. Decrease your salt use, no alcohol, minimize your caffeine intake. I'll see you in one month."

My mouth opened. I wanted to ask another question, but nothing came out. I hated my jumbled thoughts and the inability to formulate questions quickly enough. Then the tears welled up. *Heart transplant?* I cleared my throat just as he handed me a piece of paper.

By the time I had read the small rectangular prescription for Coreg CR 10 mg, I saw the back of his lab coat as he exited the room.

* * *

When I scheduled my follow-up appointment with the cardiologist, I cringed at the thought of returning to such a cold experience.

My oncologist, Dr. Schwartz, once asked how my appointments were working out with my other doctors. "Do you like them?"

"I guess."

"If you're unhappy with a physician, why don't you find a new one?"

"Ugh. Then I have to pick up my medical records and transfer them to a new office. Try doing that with four kids."

"You're hiring them to monitor your health. Find a physician who understands you and your litany of medical ailments. You can't afford treatment errors."

Direct. That's what I loved about Dr. Schwartz. He scribbled some names on a slip of paper and handed me his recommendations.

I took his advice and spent nearly a year tracking down a new cardiologist. His magazine-cover- and plaque-lined wall featured Dr. Price as one of the best cardiologists in South Florida. My apprehensions about my first visit diminished.

"Geez, you have a horrible medical history." He looked up from my chart and flipped through my new EKG and echo scans.

Well, at least he shoots straight.

He had good news, though. My new test results revealed a mild case of MVP with only one minor leaky valve, a condition many people lived normally with.

Praise God!

"Your heart decreased in size, too," Dr. Price said, almost impressed. He wasn't exactly sure why, though.

I thought I knew why. A smile grew across my face.

45

MAY 2011

Two years later, I sat in my cardiologist's office.

"Your heart is boring," Dr. Price said during my checkup as he stared at the ultrasound screen showcasing my flapping valves.

"Boring?"

"Yes, boring. Your MVP is a minor murmur now, and there's no sign of cardiomyopathy."

"No sign? Is that normal?"

Because of my erratic medical history, he didn't have an exact answer other than that my heart showed no indication of ever having the disease. It could have been the pregnancy, he said, but that's a controversial theory. Because of the chest radiation and cardiotoxic drugs and my family history of heart disease, he really didn't know. Then he said something along the lines of my heart looking mostly normal.

"You can go." He opened the examining-room door for me and walked me to the front counter. Then he said he'd see me in six months. I was certain I detected a grin.

I left his office, my face beaming. No doctor had ever used the word *normal* when describing my health. *Something about me is normal! Well, mostly normal.* Either way, I'd take it.

46

MY JOURNEY HAS BEEN a process of flipping over stones and chasing the ugliness out, because under those rocks lurked the true state of my heart. Of what I believed or who I believed in. It will always be me plugging along, surrendering, praying for wisdom, asking God to use whatever ickiness I go through. I've realized I don't need to win at this life or slay my weaknesses all at once. I just need to bring God glory, to fulfill my vow, to be usable. That was a big step in the right direction and possibly a fulfillment of God's promise that the second half of our lives would be better than the first—because I was realizing there was freedom in releasing control.

My pastor recently said that "God's gifts and his call are irrevocable" (Romans 11:29). That once God puts a calling on people's lives, they will never feel at peace until they are following his will. Then he asked, "What part of your life are you surrendering to God and allowing him to use for his Kingdom?"

I remember snickering as I shook my head. *God's been calling me all along to do the thing I never wanted to do: write.*

I spent a good portion of my life fearing death. I stressed over it, desperately clinging to the hope that my doctors would say with certainty that I'd live. I think that was a normal response, but at some point I wished someone had snipped out the part of my brain that worried so much. Because to be honest, I didn't realize how precious life is until it was threatened.

Maybe I needed my own plaque-lined wall that showcased each disease and even a nifty picture for visual effect. The header could read:

Relax. God's got this, remember? No? Well, here's a little sampling of what he's already brought you through:
- Relapse of Hodgkin's disease: survival rate 30 to 50 percent.
- Pulmonary embolism: "She'll never make it through the night."

- Risk for life-threatening hemorrhaging: "She'll experience spontaneous internal hemorrhaging."
- Acute pneumonia with a severely compromised immune system because of the stem-cell transplant.
- Acute pneumonia again: "She'll be hospitalized a minimum of a month, but be prepared that she may never leave."
- Acute Respiratory Distress Syndrome (ARDS).
- Whole-body inflammation brought on by infection and multiple organ failure (lung/kidney failure/ heart enlargement), which led to sepsis (blood poisoning) and septic shock: chance of survival 20 to 30 percent.
- Congestive heart failure.
- Severe mitral valve prolapse: severe mitral regurgitation, which will require valve repair or replacement.
- Cardiomyopathy: progressive heart enlargement and weakening over time. Good candidate for a heart transplant in the future.

Feel better? Good. *Now go tell someone about Jesus.*

Exposing my soul for the world to see has been frighteningly therapeutic, because rereading this list of medical events makes me want to shake the author and say, "Don't you see? God brought you through some crazy stuff, lady.

You survived! You had more kids. Your marriage is looking pretty decent, you wrote a book and even used some two-syllable words. Glory! Stand up and give praise to almighty God for his amazing sense of humor. Stop trying to be perfect, and save all that wasted energy for the people who look just like you, because you can spot them better than anybody else can. They may not have cutoff shorts and carry an Enfamil bag, but the despair filling their hearts looks the same on their faces."

So that's what I decided to do—push myself past my limits, knowing that one day I will be fully rested and refreshed. It might not happen until I'm jumping up and down in front of heaven's gates, but for now, I've got kids to chase, a husband to love, and some crazy stories to share with whoever will listen. Because until God takes my last breath, I'll tell of the time I did not die but lived, and "will proclaim what the Lord has done" (Psalm 118:17).

To God be all glory, forever and ever. Amen.

I love the LORD, for he heard my voice;
    he heard my cry for mercy.
Because he turned his ear to me,
    I will call on him as long as I live.

The cords of death entangled me,
    the anguish of the grave came upon me;
    I was overcome by trouble and sorrow.
Then I called on the name of the LORD:
    "O LORD, save me!"

The LORD is gracious and righteous;
    our God is full of compassion.
The LORD protects the simplehearted;
    when I was in great need, he saved me.

Be at rest once more, O my soul,
    for the LORD has been good to you.

—PSALM 116:1-7

Epilogue

WHEN MY WIFE, Dabney, was diagnosed with cancer so soon after learning that we were going to have a baby, friends, coworkers, and acquaintances often commented that such a terrible sickness and tragedy didn't make sense. Not for Dabney. She was an angel. She served God faithfully, attended every church and youth group function, volunteered, served on mission trips overseas, and had a genuinely pure heart. It just seemed cruel that God would allow the double dose of suffering through chemotherapy and radiation while we feared for the life and health of our unborn daughter Madison.

But behind the scenes, many things were happening.

Dabney and I were not happy after our first year of marriage. It was actually going steadily downhill. As twenty-one-year-old college seniors, we knew so little about marriage, and many advisors warned us that we were too young to marry. A divorced coworker at the Breakers Hotel in Palm Beach, where I served for banquets part-time, stated it bluntly: "You're about to make the most foolish decision in your whole life, and you're actually excited about it." I simply asked her how many times she had been married, and when she answered five, I ended the conversation by thanking her for making it clear *not* to take her advice. I decided at that moment that the word *divorce* would never be in our vocabulary and that I would be committed to Dabney regardless of any internal or external influences.

We both loved God, and we loved each other, but we struggled with showing it correctly. We had drastically different expectations for marriage. I thought like a male, she thought like a female. I was insensitive and capable of painfully sharp words in retaliation for her stubbornness or disrespect of me in front of our peers. I'm not sure we would have made it without God's intervening.

Something in me started to soften when I saw Dabney in pain. The more I saw her suffer, the more shame I began to feel at how I had treated her. The fairy tale most little girls have of meeting a prince and living happily ever after was not what she was experiencing. I failed to provide any of the emotional security, self-confidence, or words of affirmation that she desperately needed. I considered that if my wife succumbed to the cancer, her brief marriage experience with me would haunt me the rest of my life. I imagined watching a young man treating my own little girl as carelessly as I treated the wife I had promised to cherish only a few years earlier.

All these feelings intensified as Dabney grew more ill. The anxiety of wanting to become a better husband with perhaps only limited time to change began to cross paths with watching my wife increase in determination and strength. God began to show me so many new things to love her for. I was amazed by her pain tolerance as I watched the bone-marrow-biopsy needle pushed into her hip bone. She squeezed my hand harder the deeper the needle went in while Dr. McGarry twisted the T-handle in a circular motion to extract the core sample. I watched her fight back tears as her beautiful blonde hair started to come out in clumps when she ran her fingers through it. I saw her wincing in pain as she attempted to swallow small bites of food; Dabney equated it to swallowing razor blades because of the painful sores in her mouth from the chemotherapy. I stood by and observed how at only eighty pounds, bald with pale skin, she fought to stay alive for her daughter. I witnessed her determination as the doctors in the ICU brought her out of her chemically-induced coma long enough for her to push twice for the birth of our son and then collapse back into sleep from the fatigue. I have watched her transformation from struggling to walk to the mailbox because of her reduced lung capacity to crossing the finish line on a 5K run.

I have discovered so many reasons to admire her as God has transformed my heart permanently. I realized years later that a true heart change rarely occurs in days or weeks but over years. It took the most severe circumstances to break us both down and rebuild us the way God knew we both needed.

As Dabney mentioned, I did indeed hear from God. At that moment, I knew that we could not judge our current circumstances without knowing what God intended for our future. I knew that God promised to spare her life, and that was enough for me. What I didn't know was how much sweeter life could be after so much pain. As God continues to fulfill his promise of increasing our family, our land, our livestock (resources), I realize that I would not wish the pain of our journey on my worst enemy. Simultaneously, I realize that I would never want to trade the experience and go back to the person I was before. When someone asks, "Why does God allow bad things to happen to good people?" I know in my heart that it's because he is at work orchestrating a purpose beyond what we can see or imagine. Sometimes we see the results, sometimes not.

During Dabney's many life-threatening illnesses,

people frequently told her that she should write a book to encourage others and to share what God had done in her life. Dabney also promised God numerous times that if he would show up in a particular instance, she would be obedient and write the book. This work is a testament to God's promises, the labor of love, and my wife's commitment to obedience. May it bless you in some way on your journey as it has me in mine.

—Jason Hedegard

Acknowledgments

Many thanks to: Brett and Colleen Wilcox for opening your house; Nancy Askew for babysitting during my Moffitt treatments; Marge Sullivan for listening and letting me cry; First Baptist of Palmetto, especially Brother Mike; Calvary Church in Jupiter for your prayers and support; Ronda Hawkins for pick-me-up chicken potpies; Ragan Massey for spilling the beans and wearing a hospital mask in public—just to make me feel normal; my Facebook friends and blog followers for prayers and helpful suggestions; Mike Keller for persuading me to share my testimony, which sparked a speaking passion I never knew existed.

Lyndsey Cornell, who volunteered months of editorial time and later admitted had you not known me or my story, you never would have pushed me to continue writing because it was "that bad." Best. Fibber. Ever. God ingeniously placed you in my life during the infancy of this project. Thanks for the hand-holding.

Faith-builders and Wellington critique groups, especially Mark Adduci and Caryn Devincenti, for your optimism; Jennifer Fonseca for not holding back and Sundays at Panera; Backroom Writers group, particularly Lois Blackburn, for keeping us in line. You guys helped me grow with each reading—even when my voice wobbled.

Gretchen Cristantiello for Chick-fil-A coupons, dinners along PGA, and girlie prattling sessions when I needed them most.

Cheryl Plourde, my cheerleader of fourteen years, for telling me God would use this story long before I saw the vision and for inspiring me to write and speak and homeschool. And to your hubby, Pastor Dan Plourde, for preaching God's Word, speaking truth into my life, and reminding me that God gives each of us unique callings to reach people for the Kingdom and that we're supposed to use our God-stories to bring him glory.

I'm indebted to the doctors who aided in saving my life. To the medical institutions, especially Moffitt Cancer Center, who juggled my scariest nights. Special thanks to Dr. Theresa Field and Dr. Karen Fields for painstakingly reviewing my Moffitt chapters. Bless you, Dr. McGarry, for your stance on life. Without your support, Madison may never have been born. Thanks also to Dr. Augustin Schwartz and Dr. Richard Price. I'm glad I helped put your kids through college.

Lisa Schwartz for hiding butterfly needles for my mini-veins and Kathy Edwards for her Jesus smile and the hours spent translating my St. Mary's medical records.

My fabulous editor, Carol Traver, for liking Earl Grey, searching for me when I forgot to leave my contact information at the Writing for the Soul Conference (WFTSC), for knowing what to leave in and most certainly what to leave out. To Susan Taylor and her magic editing wand, and to the whole team at Tyndale, you've been a dream to work with.

Jerry B. Jenkins and the WFTSC for allowing newbies access to agents and editors and for teaching us tips to sway them into liking us. Special thanks to James Watkins for gingerly offering feedback.

Rachelle Gardner, my brilliant agent with Books & Such Agency—you're ah-maz-ing. Your quickly returned phone calls, encouraging words, and savvy advice helped me back to normal when I wanted to hide or run or devour fistfuls of Dutch chocolate.

My dad for being proud of me and saying so; your continued support fills my heart with joy. I love you so much.

Mom, on your knees you've prayed me through high school and illnesses and cheered me through this writing process, even when the delete button looked mighty tempting. I love you bunches.

Christine for proofing my articles, looking out for me, and treating me to personalized gifts from UncommonWares.com, which kept me fashionable. I love you, big sis.

My husband for loving on the kids while I played at my bimonthly critique or Toastmasters group, for the big shove to attend the second WFTSC, where I met with Tyndale. Had I not gone, there would be no book—well, unless you count the one I planned on creating with crayons and a three-ring binder. For supporting whatever crazy project I jumped into with childlike enthusiasm. But mostly, for your faith in God and a shoulder to lean on and a hand to hold. You're my best friend. I love you forever.

My children, who never should have been: Madison, Ansley, Asher, and Sabal, your joy-filled faces keep this mommy going, even during my slow days. God is preparing you for great things. I love you more than a ba-billion, ca-trillion (said in Sabal-speak).

Lastly, I thank the one who always supported me, who nudged me on when I dismissed this project. Each time he sent whispers of encouragement through Caryn, Lyndsey, Bryon Mondok, Nicole Oliva, my editor at the Good News, the stranger in Barnes & Noble who overheard a chapter read aloud and asked where she could buy the book. Those glimpses of hope continued until the end when he whispered in Carol's ear that this story might be worth telling. All thanks belong to God. For without him, this book never would have been written. Promise fulfilled. Thanks for the son.

About the Author

DABNEY HEDEGARD is a writer, speaker, and professional patient. When Dabney was just twenty-five, a football-sized tumor entangled vital organs in her chest and alerted doctors to the cancer attacking her body. But a greater cause of concern grew inches below the mass: a six-week-old baby. Dabney's disease and her decision to keep her child marked the beginning of her battles with nine life-threatening illnesses and four near-death experiences.

Dabney graduated from Palm Beach Atlantic University with a BA in theater. In addition to writing for the *Good News* newspaper, Dabney speaks at local churches, MOPS groups, women's conferences and crisis pregnancy centers.

She and her husband, Jason, live in South Florida with their four children and attend Calvary Church in Jupiter. Dabney enjoys interacting with readers on her website, www.dabneyland.com.